GENERAL CROOK
AND THE
SIERRA MADRE
ADVENTURE

GENERAL CROOK AND TH[E]

by Dan L. Thrapp

IERRA MADRE ADVENTURE

UNIVERSITY OF OKLAHOMA PRESS : NORMAN

By Dan L. Thrapp

Al Sieber, Chief of Scouts (1964)
The Conquest of Apacheria (1967)
General Crook and the Sierra Madre Adventure (1972)

INTERNATIONAL STANDARD BOOK NUMBER: 0–8061–0993–9

LIBRARY OF CONGRESS CATALOG CARD NUMBER: 71–177347

COPYRIGHT 1972 BY THE UNIVERSITY OF OKLAHOMA PRESS, PUBLISHING DIVISION OF THE UNIVERSITY. COMPOSED AND PRINTED AT NORMAN, OKLAHOMA, U.S.A., BY THE UNIVERSITY OF OKLAHOMA PRESS. FIRST EDITION.

For Jarvis Zeeck,

who does the finest bush flying I know,

and for Bea, who lets him.

INTRODUCTION

The purpose of this slender volume is twofold. Primarily it is an attempt to describe in detail the 1883 military expedition —the most important and dangerous United States Army operation against hostile Indians in the history of the American frontier, yet one of the least known—and to retrace the route of the expedition into the Sierra Madre of northern Mexico. The book's second purpose is to delineate the chain of events which made this undertaking necessary, in fact, inevitable.

The bold and imaginative expedition did not originate in the mind of Brigadier General George Crook, who successfully carried it out. Rather, it began long before Crook had returned to command in Arizona, with the unfortunate, bloody clash on Cibecue Creek—a diplomatic and military blunder of a magnitude unimagined at the time. From the affair on the Cibecue ensued a succession of disasters: the Juh outbreak and fights, the Loco émeute and battles, the engagement at Big Dry Wash, and the Chatto raid, until a perilous situation had developed. There formed, secure in the Sierra Madre, a pool of more than 500 Apache hostiles, including perhaps 150 warriors and boys of fighting age. As active, persistent raiders, they posed a serious threat to orderly development of the region. The idea of the Mexican expedition evolved in Crook's mind as the only viable solution to a problem which, to many of the day, appeared insoluble.

No historian has yet seen these scattered events as an integrated whole nor recognized the significance and nature of the complex causes which made the Sierra Madre expedition necessary. Similarly, no historian has described the extreme perils overcome or precisely how the expedition was conducted.

Under the masterful guidance of Crook, the Sierra Madre expedition succeeded. It made possible the effective solution to the Apache Indian problem, even if its merit and accomplishments were submerged by the flood of publicity surrounding the relatively minor Geronimo outbreak two years later. The 1883 expedition, though it made safer the mining and agricultural development of much of Arizona and New Mexico, has been, perhaps, the most neglected major accomplishment in our Southwestern history.

As I perused a newly arrived Arthur H. Clark Company catalog of Americana new, used, and rare books one evening, an entry stood out as though bordered by lights:

> 184. Bourke (John G.) An Apache Campaign in the Sierra Madre; an account of the expedition in pursuit of the hostile Chiricahua Apache in the Spring of 1883. Introduction by J. Frank Dobie. Special copy. Has . . . a large folding map of the campaign by a Lt. Freberger, not found elsewhere. Pp. 128. New York [1958].

The student of Southwestern Indian wars would know at

once that "Freberger" could have been none other than Gustav Joseph Fiebeger, a well-known army engineer officer, who, in his professional capacity, had accompanied General Crook on the remarkable expedition into the Sierra Madre, and that the map might possibly be the one compiled from his field notes of that campaign, or a copy of it. For many years I had been seeking that map, feeling certain that it would answer numerous questions about the expedition, its precise route, where it fought the Indians, on what streams it camped, and how it returned to this country with several hundred surrendered Apaches.

A telephone call, an anxious wait, and then the book and map arrived. I found the map to meet and even to surpass all expectations. While not the original, it apparently was a blueprint copy of what may have been the original. It was a sizable map, approximately 16½ by 28¾ inches, showing in finely lettered detail the precise course of the party, every camping place except one, the principal topographical features, and the crossings of the Bavispe River. It also showed the location of the fight with Chatto's and Bonito's rancherias, and the location of García's fights with Loco's band to the north of the Sierra Madre and later with entrenched Apaches on a mountaintop within that vast range.

The map opened new avenues for research, but the first question to be answered was how it came into the bookseller's hands. Investigation disclosed that it had been obtained from Lamar Moore, a retired railroad chief clerk and superintendent and a collector of Americana and a student of Southwestern cattle and Indian history. Upon retirement, Moore had disposed of a portion of his collection; among the items was the Bourke book and map.

Moore had been chief clerk in Arizona for the Atchison,

Topeka and Santa Fe Railway Company for many years, stationed at Winslow, a division point, where offices and considerable files were maintained. Several years before his retirement a new office building had been constructed. Moore wrote me:

> In preparing to move from the old building (in 1960), all old files were gone through and those of no use destroyed. Among these old files the boys in the engineering department found a copy of the Fiebeger map. From this drawing the map you now have was made. I haven't the slightest idea, and neither did anyone else, as to where this drawing came from; nor was it known if it was the original made by Fiebeger or a copy. There was nothing to show.

The problem remained, how and why did this map, or a copy of it, come into possession of the railway company? Neither Moore nor anyone in the various Southwestern offices of the system had any light to shed. One complicating factor was a cryptic statement on the chart: "Note: . . . see letter April 10–'04 Lieut Col F West to Mr J H Emmert." Among possible interpretations of this phrase was that the map still held interest for someone as late as 1904. "Lieut Col F West" was Frank West, a junior officer in the 6th Cavalry who had won a Medal of Honor at the Battle of Big Dry Wash and had been active in Arizona during much of the later Apache war days. Though at San Carlos and not on the Crook Sierra Madre campaign, he would have had much information about the expedition. But who was J. H. Emmert?

More information was forthcoming from Rudolph Henri Beeder, chief engineer of the Santa Fe System. Beeder had already investigated the matter as far as he could. Other copies of the Winslow map had reached Chicago and intrigued him because of his abiding interest in Western Americana. He wrote:

> We have copies of the extremely interesting map. Our people (at Winslow) recall that they had an ink drawing of the Crook map on tracing cloth in 1960 at the time the reproductions were made. However at this time no one at Winslow is able to locate the tracing and it is not even indexed in our map records there. I suppose we will just have to surmise that this tracing cloth map has been lost, misplaced, or perhaps has some involvement in grand larceny.

Beeder reported that Emmert "was an employe of the Santa Fe, Prescott and Phoenix Railway Company for several years. In 1899–1903 he held the position of Assistant to the President with headquarters in Prescott." However, Emmert's name was not shown in the company's eleventh annual report for the fiscal year ending June 30, 1905. Emmert had apparently left his railway position to become auditor of the Simon Murphy estate at Detroit, Murphy probably having been a director of the Santa Fe, Prescott and Phoenix Railway Company. According to Beeder:

> We do not know anything about . . . the career of Mr. Emmert after he left Prescott for Detroit, but it may be possible that the 1904 letter mentioned in the note on the map had been a part of Mr. Emmert's personal papers. We do not have any specific reason as to why the map was in our files at Winslow, except that in the early days of Santa Fe expansion one of our objectives was to serve Mexico and probably our people at Prescott and other points on the System endeavored to obtain all the information on the country that was possible.

The Santa Fe Company's interest in railroads across northern Mexico dated from the late 1860's. In 1878 a survey was

completed from Deming, New Mexico, southwesterly, cross-
ing the extreme southeastern corner of Arizona near the San
Bernardino Ranch and continuing in a straight course through
Guadalupe, Fronteras, Bocachic, and Arizpe toward Hermo-
sillo. The line eventually built, however, ran from Nogales,
Arizona, south to Guaymas, a port on the Gulf of California.
It was the inaugural trip over this new route that Crook was
invited to join late in 1882 but was forced by the press of
Indian affairs to decline. Later he did make that journey, as
related in this book.

While projecting its major west-coast line across Arizona
more or less along the 35th parallel, the Santa Fe continued
to explore the possibility of other routes. The line to Guaymas
was reconnoitered in 1867 by engineer William Raymond
Morley, although the route was not actually surveyed for
eleven more years.

When the Santa Fe reached Las Vegas, New Mexico, in
1879, it had a threefold plan. One was to go from Albuquerque
west to California. Another was to go south to Mexico City
via El Paso. A third was the determination to lay rail southwesterly to Guaymas. But by the time the Santa Fe Railroad
reached Deming, on March 20, 1881, the Southern Pacific
Company had already arrived at that point from the west.
Therefore it was arranged for the Santa Fe to use Southern
Pacific rails to Benson, Arizona, by a trackage right, and to
build its own line from Benson to Nogales, a segment completed by a subsidiary company on September 26, 1882. The
line from Benson to Guaymas, incidentally, later was transferred to the Southern Pacific in exchange for its Mojave
Division between Needles, on the Colorado River, and
Mojave, north of Los Angeles.

In a letter-report dated November 28, 1878, Santa Fe Chief

Engineer Albert Alonzo Robinson recommended to William B. Strong, general manager of the company, that construction of a line be along the 32d, rather than the 35th parallel. Robinson mustered numerous arguments to support his views. Among them was that construction of the road along the former parallel (later developed by the Southern Pacific) "will bring to the front, adventurers, who will persistently work for, and finally succeed in obtaining another 'Texas,' from the territory of Old Mexico. This will open the route to Guaymas, on the Gulf of California; will call for another through line to the Pacific, which can be built by your Company."

Thus it can be seen that the Santa Fe had an interest in northwestern Mexico for at least fifteen years prior to the Sierra Madre expedition. It must be presumed that it was this concern that led some unknown member of that firm to acquire either a copy of the map or the original itself at some time after its drafting.

The Crook map was not drawn by Fiebeger but compiled from his field notes. In a typical communication explaining this procedure, Captain John S. Loud, acting assistant adjutant general at the Headquarters of New Mexico, informed Colonel George P. Buell in early 1881:

> Your attention is respectfully invited to Gen'l Orders No. 4, series of 1878, from these Headquarters which does not require maps of scouts, but the necessary field notes for the preparation of maps. The original notes are required to be sent to these Headquarters, where the necessary maps will be prepared, in the office of the Chief Engineering Office, from the notes.[1]

[1] LS20DNM1881 Loud to Buell, Fort Stanton, January 21, 1881, in Letters Sent (LS), District of New Mexico (DNM), Record Group 393, National Archives and Records Service, Old Army Records.

In the "Report of Lieutenant G. J. Fiebeger, Corps of Engineers, for the Fiscal Year Ending June 30, 1883," written from Whipple Barracks at Prescott, Fiebeger stated that he had accompanied Crook into Mexico and that "while in the field such notes were kept as was possible under the circumstances, and rough maps of the country traversed have since been made in this office." These were refined into the finished map, Fiebeger implied.[2]

The location of the original of this map is not known. Copies are in the possession of various persons connected with the Santa Fe Railway, and one is in the University of Wyoming Historical Library, according to Mr. Moore. The Cartographic Branch of the National Archives and Records Service has a tracing, A. P. Muntz, chief of the branch, reported, but it is smaller than the copy from the bookseller, measuring 13 by 22¼ inches, and it is not an exact copy of the larger map. The latter shows more detail and is rougher in appearance, as though done by draftsmen in a preliminary way, while the smaller version is much more professional. But it takes certain liberties with the larger map, omits some of its information, although little that is substantive, and endeavors here and there to correct it. For example, the second García fight, in the mountains, is dated April 20, 1883, in the larger map, and is April 26 in the smaller, although the fight actually took place on April 25. I believe that the larger map, sold me by the bookseller, is superior. Though slightly more "primitive," the larger map is closer to the original if not, indeed, a blueprint of it, and thus better depicts the event. Neither the original for the large map nor that for the smaller version can now be located. "We can only surmise that the

<hr>

[2] *Annual Report of the Chief of Engineers, U.S. Army to the Secretary of War for the Year 1883*, Part 3, Appendix AAA, 2404–2406.

original was lost after copies were made," Muntz believes. The Archives copy is filed as AMA 273.

It would appear probable that the larger map is a blueprint of the true original, compiled at Whipple Barracks under Fiebeger's supervision, as he stated in his 1883 report. Either the first draft, or a copy of it, was sent to Washington, from which more practiced draftsmen made the smaller, polished version, a copy of which remains in the Archives. Emmert, being stationed for many years at Prescott, no doubt was acquainted with army officers at Whipple Barracks. At some time he may have learned of the existence of this map, procured a copy or perhaps even the original of it, and either this copy or a duplicate of it eventually wound up at Winslow.

Crook's 1883 endeavor was no routine scout after Apaches. As one reference work states. "Viewed from any standpoint, the expedition was one of the most extraordinary ever undertaken against the Indians."[3] By using the map, we are able finally to summarize the events of the expedition accurately and assess its true worth in the settlement of Indian troubles, a necessary precursor to peaceful settlement of much of the Southwest.

At the time Crook came into command of the Department of Arizona, there were large numbers of hard-bitten Apache warriors living more or less unmolested in the rugged, almost inaccessible Sierra Madre. To the Southwesterner, these Indians represented an immense force for evil, and there appeared to be no way in which they could be brought under control, for outright military combat was the most illusory and difficult to bring about of all possible recourses. Crook, while not shunning action of this sort, well realized this fact. It is probable that no other officer of the frontier army could

[3] *National Cyclopedia of American Biography*, IV, 71.

have so clearly assessed the problem and conceived its most viable solution while possessing the capacity to bring it about.

The campaign was the climactic one for the Apache wars of the Southwest; of that there can be little doubt. Never again, despite the headline-grabbing propensity of Geronimo and his fellows, would any important numbers of hostiles roam the area. Although a great deal of army strength was mustered to meet and solve the Geronimo threat, the depredations of that small band of hostiles were minor compared with the potential of the Sierra Madre Apaches. It was because he so well understood this threat that Crook must be regarded as the key man in solving the Indian problem of the region.

Although there have been considerable changes in Mexican life in the eighty-five years since the Crook campaign, those areas in the Sierra Madre where Crook fought, counciled, and argued with the hostiles remain virtually as they were then—remote, difficult of access, little known.

In a chartered plane I was flown over the route, as nearly as it can be picked out from the air, by my brother-in-law and the best bush pilot of my experience, Jarvis Zeeck of Plainview, Texas. The main geographical features, of course, are unchanged. The Bavispe, the Janos, and the other streams still flow as they did. The small Mexican communities, freed now from the Apache menace, are perhaps more prosperous, though they appear much as they must have to Crook, to Bourke, to John Rope, and to Al Sieber. The mountains are, by human standards, immutable. The forests of oak and pine are still vast, although cutting goes on. Here and there is a miner's camp or stockman's corral that would not have existed in Apache days. Particularly on the Janos plains to the north, there are today great ranches with their topographical modifications—tanks, buildings, fences, water ditches, and plowed fields—that are new since Loco led his horde across them from Enmedio to the Sierra Madre. Still, the flatness of the land is inviolate and the creeks, watercourses, hills, and some of the springs remain.

After the aerial reconnaissance, I traveled as much of the route as can be done on the ground by means of a rugged International Scout. For company I had splendid companions, such as James Walker of Florissant, Missouri; Philip Van Strander of Scottsdale, Arizona; Wendel Towse of Alton, Illinois; John A. (Bud) Shapard of the Bureau of Indian Affairs, then of Parker, Arizona, but now of Washington, D.C.; and Eugene Quail of St. Louis. We visited the Bavispe River towns of Huachinera, Bacerac, and Bavispe, the García fight locale (we could not locate the actual battleground, so completely have its relics disappeared in the decades since that tragic morning), and the site of the Loco fight before Enmedio Mountain, finding some of the relics of war—cartridge cases and rock breastworks—and also visiting Horseshoe Canyon where Forsyth fought Loco, and once more threading Doubtful Canyon from east to west, as the band of hostiles did in 1882. I had previously visited most of the other scenes of action, because they are more readily accessible.

These travels reinforced my admiration for the hostiles who swept this vast area so confidently and for the rugged durability of the soldiers and officers who chased them, fought them remorselessly, and, in rare instances, notably in the case of Crook himself, understood and sympathized with them. Knowing that control over the hostiles was inevitable, these soldiers brought it about, dealing honestly and kindly with the Indians, guiding them with compassion and integrity into the inexorable course that history decreed they must follow.

The assistance of many persons, of course, has helped to make this book possible. In addition to Lamar Moore, Rudolph Henri Beeder, and Jarvis Zeeck, credit must be given to Elmer O. Parker and Garry D. Ryan of the Old Military Records Division; to Richard S. Maxwell and Jane F. Smith of the Social and Economic Records Division; and A. P. Muntz, chief, Cartographic Branch, all of the National Archives and Records Service. Without their intelligent and generous help this project would have gotten nowhere.

Sidney B. Brinckerhoff, director of the Arizona Pioneers' Historical Society, and Andrew Wallace and John Bret Harte, former editors of the *Journal of Arizona History*, have listened patiently to endless reports as the work advanced and have offered valuable suggestions. Loretta Davisson of the Arizona Pioneers' Historical Society Library staff has been unendingly patient and diligent in searching out information in answer to countless requests. John L. Polich, curator in charge of the history division at the Museum of New Mexico at Santa Fe, likewise has been helpful.

Eve Ball, accomplished historian of Hollywood, New Mexico, and Clara T. Woody of Miami, Arizona, have been characteristically generous with their time and vast knowledge. James Blackburn of Pine, Arizona, who knows the central part of his state better than anyone since Al Sieber, has proven a wonderful companion on many an adventurous reconnaissance and such an unending fount of exact information about everything from hidden springs and canyons to mountain gaps, Indian remains, local history and legend, routes, trails, and other things that to do him full credit here would be impossible. The late Ruben Salazar, then the knowledgeable *Los Angeles Times* correspondent at Mexico City (in late 1970, he was tragically slain while covering a Chicano incident in East Los Angeles), helped me gain access to the reserved archives of that nation, and my gratitude goes to him and to his secretary, R. A. Bilak.

However important all of these people have been in the researching and fact-determination necessary to such a work, it goes without saying that any errors in the finished product are my own.

Whittier, California   Dan L. Thrapp
August 24, 1971

CONTENTS

ILLUSTRATIONS

MAPS

GENERAL CROOK
AND THE
SIERRA MADRE
ADVENTURE

I PRELUDE TO DISASTER

The most daring, imaginative, and one of the more successful campaigns against Indians in American frontier history had its origins in the vagaries of an ascetic wisp of an Apache medicine man—a visionary, a dreamer, an individual who desired only good for his people and who was slain for attempting to bring to them what he considered the bare bones of justice.

Noch-ay-del-klinne was this Apache. He was killed at an action on Cibecue Creek, in eastern Arizona. His death set into motion a chain of events that rocked the Southwest: repeated *émeutes*, pursuits, battles, and raids—incidents finally ended by Brigadier General George Crook's bold plunge deep into the Sierra Madre of Old Mexico, from which he hoped to lure the Apache hostiles back to their Arizona reservations and the ways of peace. Against all odds, Crook succeeded.

This is the story of that series of incidents and their culmination under the inspired leadership of the often misunderstood but nonetheless determined and able general officer.

Noch-ay-del-klinne may have been to Washington and may have enlisted as one of Crook's initial band of scouts in about 1872.[1] Whether this is true, he was important enough to be described by Post Surgeon L. Y. Loring in a report from Camp Apache three years later:

> Bobby-ti-klen-ni, about fifty years of age, is an honest sober man. He is chief of the largest subtribe which may be accounted for by his generosity and mildness. He controls his people with a steady hand, and is impartial in his dealings with both white man and Indians. At one time he was hostile, but is now well affected towards the Government.[2]

Noch-ay-del-klinne first appears prominently in the records during the fateful summer of 1881. On Sunday, June 12, Major James Biddle, 6th Cavalry, wired Colonel Orlando Bolivar Willcox, brevet Major General, commanding the Department of Arizona, from Fort Grant. He reported that Joseph Capron Tiffany, Indian agent at the vast San Carlos Apache Reservation, "thinks there might be some trouble" with his Indians. "The young bucks . . . were going to make war." Biddle added that there was "nothing alarming I think."[3] He was overly sanguine.

[1] John G. Bourke, *On the Border with Crook*, 178. Sidney B. Brinckerhoff casts doubt that Noch-ay-del-klinne ever served as a scout. Book Review, *Journal of Arizona History*, Vol. IX, No. 1 (Spring, 1968), 51. Frank C. Lockwood says the Indian went to Washington in 1871, met President Grant, and was given a medal which he wore at his death. He was described by Lockwood as thirty-six at his demise, "a slender, light-skinned, ascetic-looking man, about one hundred and twenty-five pounds in weight and less than five feet and a half in height." *The Apache Indians*, 235–36.

[2] L. Y. Loring, Surgeon U.S. Army, Camp Apache, A. T., "Report on Coyotero Apaches," January 11, 1875, Bancroft Library (quoted courtesy, the Bancroft Library, University of California, Berkeley). The name Loring gives for him is one of the many variations of this Indian's cognomen.

[3] LS2181DA1881 Willcox to Adjutant General Military Division of the Pacific, San Francisco, June 24, 1881, in Letters Sent (LS), Department of

Tiffany spoke for the Fort Apache Indians as well as his own because of an administrative decision going back five or six years. On September 23, 1875, Commissioner of Indian Affairs Edward P. Smith had informed the agent at San Carlos that "the Camp Apache Agency in Arizona, by direction of the President is discontinued, and that the Indians heretofore attached thereto will be placed under the charge of the Agent at the San Carlos Agency." Jurisdictional histories compiled by National Archives staff members indicate that the San Carlos Agency was in charge of all Apache Indians of Arizona by 1876. The Fort Apache Agency would be separated from San Carlos again, for administrative purposes, on June 7, 1897.[4]

Agent Tiffany was a key man in launching the series of incidents that led ultimately to the Crook expedition. To some extent he is a man of mystery. Much that is known of him appears to be unsavory, but proof generally is lacking as to his misdeeds, if such they were. Corruption on Indian reservations usually was tied to a desire for personal gain on the part of the individuals in a position to profit at the expense of the Indians. If Tiffany was corrupt, that fact did not appear clearly during the last years of his life. He was known to the Apaches as "Big Belly" and was said to be abrupt and even tyrannical toward them. Perhaps he was. But others have been so accused, when, by the record, they were strict dis-

Arizona (DA), Record Group 393, National Archives and Records Service, Old Army Records.

[4] Richard S. Maxwell, assistant director, Social and Economic Records Division, NARS, to author, August 19, 1968. Interior Department LS277, serial 1875, Smith to W. E. Morford, Camp Apache, September 23, 1875; LS313, serial 1875, Smith to John P. Clum, Camp Grant, A.T., September 23, 1875.

ciplinarians rather than brutal overlords. At any rate, Tiffany is an interesting individual, worthy of more complete appraisal than he can be given here.[5]

The year 1881 had seen the entire Southwest made uneasy by Indian troubles and by suspicions that such difficulties were imminent. On February 7, Colonel Edward Hatch, 9th Cavalry, commanding the District of New Mexico, urged that the number of his Indian foot scouts be increased by fifty. He also warned that "there can be no peace with the bands of hostile Indians scattered through the Territory [of New Mexico] and Northern Mexico, in small parties, until they are hunted down and exterminated."[6] He later added that even with good fortune, "it is scarcely safe to calculate upon less than a year to either kill or capture the bands now out."[7]

Hatch, a brevet major general for his distinguished Civil

[5] Tiffany was born in Baltimore, Maryland, on December 13, 1828. During the Civil War he worked, as a civilian, filling government contracts, including some for the Army of the Potomac. After the war he was investigated for suspicious practices in that job. He engaged in numerous business activities at New York and elsewhere, bringing himself to the attention of prominent and influential people. He was never a minister of the Reformed Church in America (Dutch Reformed Church), as was frequently alleged during his lifetime and after, but he was a lay member of that church and was sponsored by it when he sought the position of agent at the San Carlos agency. The Globe *Silver Belt* reported that he died at Deming, New Mexico, on July 14, 1889. The most thorough study of Tiffany's life has been done by Sidney B. Brinckerhoff, the director of the Arizona Pioneers' Historical Society. This study is incorporated in a manuscript now in preparation, "Incident at Cibicue: The Apache Uprising of 1881." Information also from Elsie B. Stryker, secretary to the Commission on History, Reformed Church in America and *Silver Belt*, July 20, 1889.

[6] LS311 District of New Mexico (DNM) 1881 Hatch to AAG, Santa Fe, February 7, 1881, Record Group 393, NARS.

[7] LS43DNM1881 AAAG, Santa Fe, to AAG, Department of the Missouri, Ft. Leavenworth, February 12, 1881.

6

War record, was a cavalryman who had once wanted to be a sailor. During the war he had taken a significant part in Ben Grierson's historic raid through the deep South. "He was an able soldier, a man of decision, firm of character and with a well-balanced judgment,"[8] but he was unfortunate in the Indians he had to fight. He had persistently chased Victorio but never caught up with him, and now he was to fail to take Nana, Victorio's most able lieutenant, as well.

A matter of prime concern to Colonel Hatch was the Southern Pacific Railroad, just built easterly from Benson, Arizona, through Willcox, Lordsburg, Deming, and to reach El Paso on May 19, 1881.[9] Hatch warned W. G. Curtis, the Southern Pacific superintendent at Tucson, that the line probably "will be subject to attacks from small depredating parties of Indians . . . from Mexico for a year to come" and that maintenance men might suffer losses. He suggested sending small troop detachments with section crews and urged "three handcars to be worked and run by soldiers to . . . patrol the road twice in every twenty-four hours" because the line passed through "a very bad Indian country."[10] Handcar cavalrymen were something new under the Southwestern sun, but Hatch was willing to try it.

In March, Hatch warned anew of the pool of hostiles in Old Mexico, saying that "we must continue to look for raids from that quarter." He urged the stationing of a small party of cavalrymen at Lake Palomas, Chihuahua, but doubted that this would be feasible because "the Mexicans were extremely sensitive" about it.[11] One month later, Hatch noted

8 *Dictionary of American Biography*, VIII, 392.

9 Neill C. Wilson and Frank J. Taylor, *Southern Pacific: The Roaring Story of a Fighting Railroad*, 77.

10 LS46DNM1881 Hatch to Curtis, February 14, 1881.

11 LS95DNM1881 Hatch to AAG, Fort Leavenworth, March 11, 1881.

that Colonel Joaquin Terrazas, the nemesis of Victorio, was scouting with about one hundred men in the vicinity of Janos, covering the routes most often taken by the hostiles in passing between Mexico and the States.[12] Despite hard scouting in all three regions, Apache difficulties seemed to increase.

On May 16, Second Lieutenant John F. Guilfoyle was sent from Fort Cummings, northeast of Deming, to the Sacramento Mountains, east of the Río Grande, to "hunt down some small bands of hostile Indians who are annoying the settlements" in the vicinity.[13]

Then, early in July, came one of the swift and destructive Apache raids which occurred repeatedly during those years. It was foreshadowed by the report that a party of engineers had been killed in the Candelaria Mountains, south of El Paso, and that the hostiles who did this were moving in the direction of New Mexico.[14]

These hostiles were a group of about fifteen former Warm Springs Apaches under old Nana, a superannuated war leader of perhaps seventy years. They crossed the border and, on July 17, collided with Guilfoyle's command in the Sacramentos, with no important loss to either side. Joined by some twenty-five Mescaleros from the Fort Stanton Reservation,[15] the raiders worked westward, clashing with Guilfoyle and other military commands ten or twelve times. They killed many whites and stole much stock, then slipped below the border again sometime after August 19, following a disastrous

[12] LS153DNM1881 Hatch to AAG, Fort Leavenworth, April 19, 1881.

[13] LS199DNM1881 Loud to Guilfoyle, May 16, 1881.

[14] LS292DNM1881 Hatch to AAG, Fort Leavenworth, July 8, 1881.

[15] This was the correct name for the Mescalero Reservation at this time. It progressed southerly from the Fort Stanton military reserve. See Charles C. Royce, "Indian Land Cessions in the United States," B.A.E. *Eighteenth Annual Report*, 882.

engagement in which they killed Second Lieutenant George Washington Smith, a brevet lieutenant colonel, and about half of his command.[16]

However spectacular Nana's raid, it was an aberration. Still, it served to remind the frontier of the considerable capacity of the Apaches, particularly those based in the Sierra Madre, to create chaos north of the border whenever they chose. Thus the implications of the raid were greater than its physical effects. But if the Nana raid was but an incident, this was not true of the developing Cibecue affair.

By early August the situation among the Indians living on the huge White Mountain (or Camp Apache) Reservation[17] had become unsettling. Colonel Eugene Asa Carr had been ordered to command Fort Apache, the heart of the troubled area, on May 30.[18] He found enough turmoil developing there to test his capacities to the limit.

A brevet major general, holder of the Medal of Honor, and an Indian fighter of considerable experience, Carr was a competent officer; his distinguished army record to this time was without important blemish. Like many frontier officers, he

[16] *Chronological List of Actions, &c., with Indians, from January 1, 1866, to January, 1891*, 51–52; *Record of Engagements with Hostile Indians Within the Military Division of the Missouri, from 1868 to 1882*, 99–100; LS330DNM1881 Hatch to AAG, Fort Leavenworth, August 5, 1881; LS415DNM1881 Hatch to AAG, Fort Leavenworth, October 3, 1881; 492AGO1881 Pope to Sheridan, August 13, 1881.

[17] This vast Indian reservation, which presently contains 1,664,872 acres, is today called the Fort Apache Indian Reservation. It was created by Executive Order on November 9, 1871, and modified by various subsequent orders. It is adjoined on the south by the San Carlos Reservation, today encompassing 1,877,216 acres. The San Carlos Reservation was created by Executive Order on December 14, 1872, to replace the Camp Grant Reservation, which had been created in 1871. See Royce, "Indian Land Cessions in the United States," B.A.E. *Eighteenth Annual Report*, 854, 860, and indicated maps.

[18] LS395MDP1883 Special Orders 60, Whipple Barracks, May 30, 1881.

cared little for Indians, nor thought much about them except as foes to be whipped or, if at "peace," as rascals to be closely watched. Until this time he had not seen much fighting on the Southwestern frontier.

He was under average height and wore a full beard which was increasingly shot with gray. Though a brave man, Carr was not above a "slow-down" (it was not called that in his day) to make a detested superior look bad in a rough situation. Carr was said to hold the loyalty of his junior officers and the affection of his men, but his relations with his superiors could be another matter.

He was extraordinarily solicitous of his own comfort, and his pride was easily injured. When something touched either of these sensibilities, he might compose windy, plaintive arguments, laying his side exhaustively in view. No doubt they were wearying to those who had to read them through, but they are a godsend to historians. He developed and maintained a long, acrimonious dispute with Willcox that did little credit to either of them, although the succession of communications takes the student behind the scenes of nineteenth-century military life as could few other documents.[19]

On August 4, Carr messaged department headquarters at Fort Whipple, outside Prescott, reporting that Noch-ay-del-klinne had been holding dances on Cibecue Creek for two months "with the object of raising from the dead Indians who have been killed." Carr stated that the medicine man "had not succeeded; but has had communications with the spirits of some of the dead Indians." Charles Hurrle, who had been hired the first of the month as interpreter,[20] warned Carr that

---

[19] For an objective study of Carr's life and career, see James T. King, *War Eagle: A Life of General Eugene A. Carr.*

[20] LS231DA1881 Benjamin to Willcox August 1, 1881. Hurrle, about whom

the Indian complained that the dead could not rise "because of the white people; that when the white people leave the dead will return and that the whites will be out of the country when the corn gets ripe" (late August or early September). Carr added that "Hurrle thinks his [Noch-ay-del-klinne's] next move may be to try to induce the Indians to hasten the departure of the whites; and that he may be working them up to a frame of mind suitable for the purpose." The officer added that friendly Indians were moving in close to the post because they were afraid of their enemies, and that there were rumors of uneasiness among the Navahos to the north, the Navahos being first cousins to the Apaches.[21]

Dances such as Carr reported seem not definitely connected with, but parallel manifestations of the so-called ghost dances, which had their origin about 1870 with the Paiutes in Nevada and culminated in 1890 with the Sioux tragedy at Wounded Knee.[22] The phenomena had obvious Christian implications.

little is known, was a key figure in the Cibecue incident. The full extent of his comprehension of the difficult Apache tongue is uncertain.

[21] 1589WD1883 (970AGO1883) in microfilm collection called *Apache Troubles 1879–1883*, Adjutant General's Office, Record Group 94, NARS, hereafter cited as AT plus serial number, such as AT159WD1883. The excerpts here are from Appendix D of the above document, dated Fort Apache August 8, 1881. William H. Carter states that the unrest had spread to all the White Mountain Apache rancherias, and that tizwin, the native Indian brew made from fermented corn (proscribed by the white authorities) had a part in the growing uneasiness. *From Yorktown to Santiago with the Sixth Cavalry*, 211.

[22] James Mooney believes the Apaches were not involved in the major ghost-dance craze, although the parallels are clearly evident. *The Ghost-Dance Religion and the Sioux Outbreak of 1890*, 49. In this connection, see also "The Medicine-Men of the Apache," B.A.E. *Ninth Annual Report*, 505, where John Gregory Bourke writes: "The Apache medicine-man, Nakay-do-klunni, called by the whites 'Bobbydoklinny,' exercised great influence over his people at Camp Apache, in 1881. He boasted of his power to raise the dead, and predicted that the whites should soon be driven from the land. He also drilled the savages in a peculiar dance, the like of which had never been seen among

In fact, Noch-ay-del-klinne, the Apache "prophet," stated on various occasions that he had been influenced by Christian teachings in the East.[23]

Tiffany, the agent from San Carlos, wired Carr on August 10 that an Indian informant had said the dancers would try again, "and if the dead did not come up it was because of the whites and they must go."[24] Carr replied on the same day that his chief of scouts, Sam Bowman,[25] had warned that the enlisted scouts were becoming affected by the dances and might mutiny. Bowman, said Carr, had gone "to have a look." On his return Bowman had accosted Second Lieutenant Thomas Cruse, in command of the scout company, and had resigned because he believed that "that kind of dance always meant trouble . . . and he didn't want to get mixed up in it."[26] Tiffany wired Carr that "it would be well to arrest Nockay-delklinne and send him off or have him killed without arresting." He added that he had informed Colonel Willcox, as well as Biddle and Hatch, of the developments. In addition, Tiffany said, he had sent emissaries to the camps of Juh, Nachez, and Chatto, war leaders of the hard-nosed Chiricahua–Warm Springs Apaches then living on the San Carlos Reservation, to sound them out.[27]

---

them. The participants, men and women, arranged themselves in files, facing a common center, like the spokes of a wheel, and while thus dancing hoddentin [corn pollen] was thrown upon them in profusion."

[23] Thomas Cruse, *Apache Days and After*, 93–94.

[24] AT1589WD1883, appendix E.

[25] Bowman, once described by Britton Davis as part Negro and part Choctaw, was an important figure in the Apache events of the early 1880's. Brave and reliable, he was said to have been murdered a few years later.

[26] Cruse, *op. cit.*, 95.

[27] AT1589WD1883, appendix G.

Willcox took a serious view of the situation. He was a serious man. Intelligent, with a high brow and lush whiskers in the fashion of the day, and with much military experience, Willcox's administrative talents were better suited to established posts and routines than to the turbulent frontier Department of Arizona where hard, quick decisions and decisive action were at a premium. Willcox had entered West Point before the Mexican War. He graduated in time to see service in Mexico City as an artillery officer and later in hostilities against the Seminole Indians in the Florida swamps. He was captured in the first battle of Bull Run, but was exchanged, and his record during the rest of the Civil War was excellent. After that conflict, he "retired" briefly to practice law and write novels, then rejoined the army as colonel of the 29th Infantry. He was transferred to the 12th, and was assigned to command the Department of Arizona on March 5, 1878. Willcox was competent, honest, and sagacious but was inclined to be verbose. His knowledge of, and empathy for the Apaches unfortunately was limited.

On August 13, Willcox messaged Carr a directive to arrest the medicine man "if you deem it necessary," after consultation with Tiffany.[28] In relaying this communication to Tiffany for his advice, Carr confessed frankly, "I do not know whether it would prevent or cause trouble to arrest him." He said he would attempt it a week later, should Noch-ay-del-klinne come to the vicinity of the post to hold another dance, as expected. "The Indians here say they expect all the Chiricahuas and Coyoteros here for the dance, which will be four or five hundred bucks, and I may not be

[28] Carr to AAAG Willcox Headquarters in the Field, November 4, 1881, *ibid.*, Appendix K.

able to arrest the Chief in the midst of that number. It might bring on instead of prevent trouble."[29] Earlier Carr had said that his total garrison at Fort Apache was 153 men.[30]

Tiffany urged Carr to lure the medicine man into the post and then arrest him. Carr answered that this might be difficult, but that he would do it if the medicine man came, "if you say so." Carr then added, "Please say clearly whether you want him arrested and how." At 9 p.m. August 14, Tiffany sent the fateful reply: "I want him arrested or killed or both."[31]

In addition to this reply was a communication from Willcox to Carr, dated from Whipple Barracks August 13, but received at 7:50 p.m. the following day. It informed Carr that Willcox desired him to "arrest the Indian doctor . . . as soon as practicable," and it reported troop movements in Arizona and New Mexico in support of Carr's anticipated operation.[32]

Carr himself, reflecting on an added complication, warned his men in a post order on August 17 that he had heard that "some silly or evil disposed soldiers have been telling the Indians that we have sent for reinforcements and cannon and intend to move the Indians off the Reservation or to attack them or to do them some harm and have been bragging what we will do to them." He said that any soldier "so foolish or wicked" should be abundantly discouraged by his comrades since "whatever the wish of a military man for war, it is his duty as a citizen as well as a servant of the nation to do nothing to bring it on."[33]

29 *Ibid.*
30 *Ibid.*, appendix F.
31 *Ibid.*, appendices M, N.
32 *Ibid.*, appendix O.

14

One more portentous incident occurred. The always unde-
pendable telegraph line, linking Fort Apache over more than
seventy-five miles of rugged mountains, desert, and canyons
with San Carlos, Fort Thomas, and Whipple, broke down
completely on August 15. Service was not restored until mid-
September. First Lieutenant William H. Carter thought Indians had cut it, but more probably the break occurred in-
nocently.[34]

Thus, before his fight on the Cibecue, Carr failed to receive another directive from Willcox: "You are authorized to
make such changes in the Scouts as may be necessary, but
will exercise discretion and not suffer the disaffected scouts
to join the malcontents."[35] Nor did Carr receive word of the
latest movement of various commands into positions of support, should he require them.

Carr's situation was not an enviable one. He was isolated
from the outside except for slow communication by mail. His
garrison was of limited size, and his scouts were suspected of
plotting mutiny. Furthermore, Carr's own soldiers had stirred
up the Apaches needlessly by their ceaseless banter, leaving
hundreds of Indians deeply moved and spurred to a near-
frenzy of expectation, exultation, and hostility. Finally, he
was in receipt of orders to move forty-six miles northwest,
enter the medicine man's camp itself, arrest him or kill him,
and return safely to his post if he could.

Carr was a resolute soldier and a competent officer of much
experience, but it is probable he never was so isolated in command, nor faced a difficult situation beset with more problems, than in this case. Still, his orders were plain. Thus, he set

[33] *Ibid.*, appendix D, quoting Post Order 125, Serial 1881, Fort Apache.
[34] Carter, *From Yorktown to Santiago*, 211.
[35] AT1589WD1883, appendix Q-1.

about carrying them out, totally unaware, of course, that the events he would set in motion would gather momentum and be climaxed two years later far south of the border in the remote mountains of Mexico.

II ACTION ON THE CIBECUE

Carr had anticipated Noch-ay-del-klinne's arrival to conduct dances hard by Fort Apache, but the prophet had not come. He had then sent two trusted scouts, Mose and Chopeau, to the Indian's camp on Tuesday, August 23, to tell the medicine man to come in by Friday morning. But the prophet was evasive and failed to make an appearance. On Monday, August 29, 1881, therefore, Carr mustered Troops D and E, 6th Cavalry, and moved out.[1]

[1] Unless otherwise cited, this summary of the Cibecue action and the attack on Fort Apache, rests upon three basic accounts: Carr's full report, dated from Fort Apache November 2, 1881: AT1589WD1883 (970AGO1883), Carr to AGO, "Official History of Operation Under Gen. Carr In and Leading Up to Cibicu Affair"; Cruse, *Apache Days and After*, 93–145, the reminiscences of the scout commander on that occasion; and Carter, *From Yorktown to Santiago*, 210–21, written by Carr's aide who won a Medal of Honor for his part in the affair. The action has frequently been described in detail. See King, *War Eagle*, 196–215; Dan L. Thrapp, *The Conquest of Apacheria*, 217–30.

The probable site was located by James Walker and others, including myself, with metal detectors, about two hundred or three hundred yards south of the present bridge across Cibecue Creek. Cartridge cases and other evidence showed that the Indians occupied what was called "Battleground Ridge" north of the sawmill on the west side of the creek, while Carr's command was centered on the bench between the creek and the highway east of the stream and almost directly opposite the ridge, though slightly upstream.

The force consisted of Colonel Carr in command; Captain Edmund C. Hentig, commanding Troop D; First Lieutenant William Stanton, commanding E; Lieutenant Carter, quartermaster and adjutant; Lieutenant Cruse, commanding Company A, Indian Scouts; and Assistant Surgeon George McCreery. Hentig's troop included 46 soldiers and Stanton's, 33. Cruse had 23 scouts of doubtful loyalty. John Byrne, whom Carr called "Burns," was guide; Hurrle was interpreter; Charles (Nat) Nobles was chief packer; and there was a *cargador*, who was assistant chief packer; 4 other packers; Carr's son, fifteen-year-old Clark M. Carr; and 9 civilians, whose names are not now known. The aggregate was 117, leaving 2 officers, 67 soldiers, and a number of civilians at Fort Apache.

The command moved "leisurely" and camped after twenty-nine miles in the deep gorge of Carrizo Creek, below the "steep and rocky sides."

"Ammunition had for two or three weeks been kept from the Indian scouts," reported Carr, because of their doubtful loyalty, but "after supper at Carrizo, ammunition was issued" to them. For this Carr later was criticized in many quarters. Major General Irvin McDowell, commanding the Division of the Pacific, of which the Department of Arizona was a part, said,

> The temper of his Indian scouts being such as to make it his duty to disarm them, thus causing them to feel that they were distrusted; the belief in their disposition to treachery being general, and that they could only be relied on till the next pay day; it was injudicious, as events have shown, in Colonel Carr to take them, with arms in their hands, to aid him in the arrest of one of their own leaders.[2]

[2] Report of Major General Irvin McDowell, commanding Military Division

But Carr, the man on the spot, felt he could do no other. Cruse said he had been asked by Carr before the expedition left whether to take the scouts and had assured the colonel that he could not find the medicine man without them. "The scouts have always been loyal, and I really believe that they will prove trustworthy," he had assured his superior.

Carr said, "I had to take the chances—they were enlisted soldiers of my command, for duty, and I could not have found the Medicine man without them." He added, "I deemed it better also that if they should prove unfaithful it should not occur at the Post," many women and children being there.

Carr called in his scouts the evening of August 29 and had a long talk with them, explaining the difficulties caused by the prophet's failure to come in to the fort. Mose, the scout who had gone to try to talk Noch-ay-del-klinne in, "manfully defended his friend," said Carr, but at length agreed that misunderstandings should be discussed in person. He suggested, and Carr approved, that he go in advance to tell Noch-ay-del-klinne the purpose of the expedition, assure him he would not be harmed, "but that he must come when sent for." Carr left Carrizo Creek early on August 30.

"Next morning the command toiled slowly up the narrow trail to the top of the canyon, and crossed the divide," wrote Carter. "Upon arriving in the valley of the Cibicu, the scouts took the trail leading along the creek, but General Carr chose the fork leading along the high open ground." This was a normal military precaution against ambush.

Sanchez, a White Mountain Apache considered a chief by most whites and a "renegade" by Cruse, rode down the col-

of the Pacific, to the General of the Army, October 1, 1881, including in Sherman's *Annual Report* for 1881, 141.

19

umn on his white horse, counting the men, as Carr and Carter believed. "It was my policy to show no distrust," the colonel reported. Then Sanchez cantered off, and other Indians inspected the troopers. The command crossed the stream and was guided to Noch-ay-del-klinne's brush wickiup.

Here occurred the critical moments of the expedition—a climactic point in this phase of Southwestern history.

Carr said he found the prophet standing in front of his lodge with the scout, Mose. The colonel continued:

> I told him through the Interpreter what I had come for. . . . This was told him in the presence of the other Indians, in their own language, so that all should understand. There were fifteen or twenty male Indians around, besides the scouts. I then told him I would treat him as a friend till those charges had been investigated and if not true he would be released. . . . I told him the agent wanted me to bring him in to talk, &c. . . . I then ordered a guard detailed; told him he was in charge of that Sergeant, [John F.] MacDonald, Troop E, 6th Cavalry; that if he tried to escape he would be killed. He smiled and said he did not want to escape, he was perfectly willing to go.
>
> I then told him that if there was an attempt at rescue he would be killed. He smiled at that also, and said no one would attempt to rescue him. I also told him he could take part of his family along with him.
>
> This talk was all in presence of other Indians, purposely to reassure them, and make a good case to their minds. Mose at times repeated and explained, when he did not seem to catch the meaning of Interpreter Hurrle.
>
> I thought that the possession of his person, as a hostage, would make them particularly careful not to bring on a collision.

One apparent key to the clash that followed lies in Carr's

admission that Hurrle had difficulty in making Noch-ay-del-klinne understand what was to be done with him and what was transpiring. Many of the conflicts of the frontier had as their origin misunderstandings on the part of either red men or white of the actual words and attitude of the other. This seems likely to have been such a case. The veteran, highly respected chief of scouts, Al Sieber, said as much a decade later in a newspaper interview. The reporter wrote, presumably on the basis of information from Sieber, that the Cibecue trouble "was caused by misinterpretation through ignorance, the interpreter not knowing enough of the Indian language," and, later, "the interpreter made a fatal blunder and the Indians getting an erroneous impression of what was intended, became greatly excited and the scouts joining them they attacked the whole command."[3]

The Reverend Francis J. Uplegger, a German-born Wisconsin Synod Lutheran missionary for forty-five years at San Carlos, compiled a unique dictionary of the Apache language, six pounds in manuscript, which now is preserved at the Huntington Library. Commenting on the intricacies and difficulties of the tongue, he described Apache as a "tone language," with up to sixty vowels and a consonant register of thirty sounds, many of them foreign to European languages. Each vowel indicates a mental picture, and the "glides" from one tone to another, "often unnoticeable to the non-Apache ear," add to a copious vocabulary and the difficulty in mastering it. "In fact," Uplegger continued, "with its wealth of word stems or roots, there is no limit to the easy formation of new words," and a very complex thought can be conveyed by a single word.[4] Thus translation between English

---

[3] *Arizona Enterprise*, Tucson, May 12, 1892.
[4] *Los Angeles Times*, June 27, 1964.

and Apache was difficult, and it is no wonder that Hurrle made mistakes, if, in fact, he did err.

Carter makes no mention of translation difficulties, but Cruse, at the wickiup with his scouts, and standing in the presence of Noch-ay-del-klinne during the interview, does so. He writes:

"Tell him," the General ordered his interpreter, "that no harm will come to him unless he or his people resist my command."

Noch-ay-del-klinne listened intently. So did the Indians gathered around.

"Say I cannot go now," the Medicine Man told the interpreter. "I have matters of importance to settle before leaving this place. Say that if the soldiers will go back to their post I will follow soon—within three or four days."

General Carr shook his head when the interpreter translated this.

"No," he answered flatly. "That will not do. Tell him that he comes with me—now."

We had been watching, listening, during the colloquy. When Carr's ultimatum was understood by the Apaches, I could actually *feel* the stiffening of that crowd, Indian by Indian. I thought the clash was coming then. The soldiers tensed in their saddles. They felt the strain too.

But my Sergeant, Mose, with some other Indians, stepped quickly over to Noch-ay-del-klinne and began to talk, reassuring him, speaking so that the other Indians of the Medicine Man's following could hear. I saw them relax and I drew a breath of relief.

It will be seen from the foregoing that the Apaches apparently had received an unsettling impression from the interpreter's translation of Carr's statements, and were reassured, for some reason, by what Mose said. It also is worth noting what General McDowell commented later, in view of Tiffany's (with the concurrence of other individuals) unreasoning suspicion that the Apaches were plotting mischief, their plans well advanced. McDowell wrote:

> However imperative may have been the necessity for the arrest of the medicine man, it was plain from Colonel Carr's notes, that the White Mountain Apaches were taken by surprise when he marched from the fort with the bulk of his command to arrest him. Those notes show that they had been disturbed by idle, mischievous, and false reports; were apprehensive of danger from the troops; uneasy and restless, but not then hostile. The fact of the troops finding the medicine man with his people in their homes, where they had been planting corn, shows that whatever may have been their ulterior plans, they were not *then* for war. . . .
>
> I cannot concur, therefore, in denouncing their conduct as treacherous. . . . These Indians simply made war upon the troops in retaliation for the arrest of their leader.[5]

Carr, after making arrangements for the medicine man to be brought along, about-faced his command so that Hentig's Troop D, which had been in the rear, now was in front, and Stanton's Troop E, which had led the march to Cibecue, brought up the rear. The pack train was between the two companies. The scouts, with the pack train, preceded Stanton's unit. Because of high brush along the creek bottom, Carr did not notice that a considerable gap developed between elements of his command, for which a court of inquiry later criticized him,[6] but the separation did not contribute to the clash nor affect its outcome in any event.

Cibecue Creek at this point winds down a rather broad val-

---

[5] Major General Irvin McDowell, *Annual Report, op. cit.*, 140–41.

[6] AT4835AGO1882 General Orders (no number), AGO, Washington, D.C., October (no date), 1882. This document, while criticizing Carr for allowing

ley, between low benches and is not in a canyon or deep basin.

Carr selected a camp ground one-quarter of a mile below the present trading post at Cibecue. He and Captain Hentig congratulated themselves that all had gone so well. Carr said he was "rather ashamed to have come out with all this force to arrest one poor little Indian. Captain Hentig . . . evidently considered it a case of great cry and little wool."

The horsemen came in, unsaddled, and turned their animals over to the herd guard, seven men including a sergeant. The pack mules arrived, were unloaded, and the packs and pack-saddles arranged in a square barricade. The medicine man was placed under guard within it. Carr reported: "My tent was nearly pitched when it was reported to me [by Cruse] that armed Indians were crowding into camp with the rear guard, and I told Capt. Hentig, who was Officer of the Day, to keep them out; he stepped towards them, waved his hands, and said 'Ucashay,' which means 'go away'."

Carter wrote that mounted Indians "coming up the creek from the gulches . . . were collecting around the Medicine Man's guard. . . . General Carr told Captain Hentig to quietly warn the Indians away from the camp and directed Lieutenant Carter . . . to separate the scouts and put them in camp. . . . Lieutenant Carter called the scouts and directed Sergeant 'Dead Shot' to put them in camp. The scouts left the other Indians, but appeared uneasy."

---

the interval to develop between elements, noted that he had given orders against such an event, although "as commanding officer he must be held responsible." It added that Carr had behaved well when the clash came, but should have kept his men under arms until his camp was established. It also said that Carr "acted wisely in taking with him the company of Indian scouts when under suspicion of disloyalty." It said Carr's errors "seem to have been those of judgment only" and complimented him for his "gallant conduct" when the action commenced.

Carr reported that Dead Shot had said, "Too much ant hills," where he was directed to camp, and Carter replied, "then go beyond the ant hills." Then, wrote Carter, "a half-witted young buck fired and gave the war cry. The long-delayed explosion took place."

Carr added that in addition to the "half-witted young buck," Dead Shot also gave the war cry, "and the scouts and all commenced firing. Sanchez went for the herd, and drove it away, killing Pvt. [John] Sonderegger."

Captain Hentig and his orderly, Edward D. Livingston, were slain at the first volley. According to Carter, "General Carr walked calmly towards the position just vacated by the mutinous scouts, and called firmly to the guard, 'Kill the Medicine Man!'" "Sergeant McDonald [*sic*], who was in charge of the guard, fired, wounding Nockay det Klinne through both thighs, but the sergeant was immediately shot by the scouts. The Medicine Man and his squaw endeavored to reach the scouts, the Messiah calling loudly to the Indians to fight, for if he was killed he would come to life again." When the firing started, the medicine man commenced crawling through the pack barricade, apparently seeking to join the hostiles. MacDonald, although himself wounded, shot him, but did not stop him, and Trumpeter William O. Benites, Carter's orderly, rammed his pistol into the prophet's mouth "while the Medicine Man was yelling," and fired, this bullet stunning, but not killing the Indian. "The squaw," recalled Carter, "was allowed to pass out of the camp chanting a weird death song in her flight."

"The Indians, as soon as they fired, which fire was at once returned by all of 'D' Troop, and all about Hd. Qrs., who could seize their guns, dodged into the brush and weeds, and got behind the trees &c. in the creek bottom, and poured a mur-

derous fire into camp," reported Carr. "It was then that
Privates Wm. Miller and John Sullivan were killed and Privates Henry C. Bird, Thomas F. Foran, and Ludwig Baege, wounded (the two former since died) all of Troop 'D' 6th Cavalry."

Stanton's troop, coming into camp last, charged dismounted through the underbrush, driving the Indians out of the bottom and cleared the area "very quickly." Stanton's efficient action had "saved the day," according to Colonel Carr, who also reported, with pardonable pride, "my son behaved very well."

"Sanchez and a few followers shot the herder nearest the stream and with wild yells, stampeded such horses as had been turned loose," Carter related.

"The firing continued until dark," continued Carr. "My tent was struck a number of times, one box of canned stuff in a breastwork was riddled and the cans set leaking. As night fell I questioned the officers, guide, chief packer &c. and found that my command was pretty unanimous in the wish 'to get out of there.' I saw no object in remaining." He ordered a "broad grave to be dug under my tent," the bodies carefully marked and placed in it, the Colonel said over them "as much of the service as I could remember, and had Taps sounded. This served for 'good night' to them and also to indicate to Indians that we were going to sleep. To fire volleys over the grave would have been to notify Indians that we were burying them at night with the intention of moving at once."

Carter said that Carr, before leaving, ordered him

to examine the body of the Medicine Man and determine if life was extinct. Strange to say, notwithstanding his wounds, he was still alive. The recovery of the Indian, if left in the hands of his friends, would have given him a commanding influence over this

26

superstitious people, which would have resulted in endless war. General Carr then repeated the order for his death, specifying that no more shots should be fired. Guide Burns [*sic*] was directed to carry out the order with the understanding that a knife was to be used. Burns, fearing failure, took an ax and crushed the forehead of the deluded fanatic.[7]

In addition to the officer and six men killed or mortally wounded, the command lost forty-five horses and ten mules killed, wounded, or missing.[8] Carr heatedly denied a rumor that he lost five thousand rounds of ammunition, but admitted losing three thousand rounds, although he said that "no ammunition nor arms which could be found were left serviceable on the field; all were destroyed or carried in some way." Nevertheless, the ammunition lost was a windfall for the Apaches, notoriously prodigal in their use of it and often finding it in short supply.

Despite doubts in various quarters as to the wisdom of the Cibecue operation, Carr reflected in his summary that

[7] Paul I. Wellman has a gory version in which Sergeant John A. Smith finishes off Noch-ay-del-klinne with ax-blows. *The Indian Wars of the West*, 413.

This account, at variance with Carter's personal-experience narrative, apparently is based on Smith's own story, as told by Anton Mazzanovich, in *Trailing Geronimo*, 124–25. It is interesting that Smith asked Mazzanovich not to make his story public, *ibid.*, 19. Wellman embellished Smith's story, and King, in *War Eagle*, 211, apparently uses Wellman's version, but with no attribution. The army assigned officers to ascertain as nearly as possible those Apaches who committed hostile acts on the Cibecue and in related incidents, and lists of their names are preserved. Eve Ball, a reliable historian who has interviewed in depth scores of the descendants of the Warm Springs and Chiricahua bands, reports that the whites started the shooting, and that Geronimo, Juh, and others of the Chiricahuas were involved. This is not confirmed by army investigators who apparently concluded that the Chiricahuas had nothing directly to do with the incident. Eve Ball, "Cibicu, an Apache Interpretation," in *Troopers West*, ed. by Ray Brandes, 121–33.

[8] McDowell, *Annual Report, op. cit.*, 143.

I now think, taking all things into consideration, and notwithstanding the losses suffered, that it was best that the arrest was made. I believe that there was already a settled determination on the part of the Indians, or that they were just coming to it, to go to war this winter. . . . Had [the Prophet] been allowed to perfect his plans and draw together the Indians still wavering or not yet under his influence, perhaps including the Navajoes and then to strike decisive and unexpected blows in every direction the disasters might have been incomparably greater.

The command left the scene of death, treachery, and destruction at 11 P.M., marching through the night over unfamiliar trails. The column reached Fort Apache at 3 P.M. on August 31.

"I found very great alarm and apprehension here," Carr conceded. No wonder. His command had been reported totally destroyed, according to rumors brought in by Mickey Free and Severiano, both former captives of the Apaches and at home with the Indians. With the telegraph line still out, Tiffany heard a report that "an Indian named Mickey" had asserted Carr and his command had been killed or trapped beyond hope of escape. Biddle reported from Camp Thomas on September 2 that

Stirling [Albert D. Sterling], Chief of Scouts at Agency, saw Mickey Free who was there at the fight, but come right in. He says Medicine Man was arrested by a Lieutenant, supposed to be Cruse. Medicine Man's brother said, "Shant arrest my brother" and killed Cruse. Troops killed Medicine man. Scouts close to troops poured their fire into them killing most of the officers and a great many men. Then the Massacre took place. A few got away holding together and trying to fight their way back to Apache. Pedro's band attacked Apache.[9]

[9] AT5843AGO1881 Biddle to AAAG, Department of Arizona in the Field, October 13, 1881, including cited dispatch, September 2, 1881, to AAG, Whipple.

Carr, in his summary report, said that "Serviana," or Severiano, "living with the Indians and now a Chief," and an Apache named Notzin had brought in the exaggerated report. News wires carried the story across the nation, rewriting it on the basis of "Custer's Last Stand. As everyone knows, that is a thrilling story," commented Cruse dryly.

If there was confusion among the whites, there was equal or greater uncertainty among the Indians. Pedro's band of White Mountain Apaches, one of the most determinedly peaceful, had become excited and some members of it may have joined the hostiles, although 32 men, 105 women, and 67 children hastily withdrew to the vicinity of the ranch of Corydon E. Cooley, forty-five miles north of Fort Apache. They stayed there, out of trouble and beyond the tempest.

Rampaging Indians, in retaliation for the slaying of their prophet, or for other reasons, cut down Privates Peter Bladt and E. Hinkler, ferrymen at the Black River crossing, a dozen miles south of the fort, and Private John Dorman, sent by Major Neville A. Cochran that morning to bring them in. Three civilians, traveling with a wagon on that same road, also were slain, as was a Mr. Cullen on Turkey Creek, a tributary of the Black. Other whites were killed in Pleasant Valley, according to Carr.[10]

These were preliminary to the next major action, which was directed against Fort Apache itself, one of the very few times in Western frontier history that an enemy attack was directed at a military establishment.

Fort Apache, on the southwestern slope of the White Moun-

---

[10] See Dan L. Thrapp, *Conquest of Apacheria*, 229–30. The slaying of two men at the Middleton Ranch in Pleasant Valley was told by an eyewitness, Hattie Middleton, in *Frontier Times*, June, 1928, and reprinted in *True West*, Vol. XI, No. 4 (March–April, 1964), 28, 48, 50.

tains at an altitude of about six thousand feet, had been established more than a decade earlier. It has not been a military post now for nearly half a century, but the outline of the army layout is still visible, and some of the old buildings remain, including a log cabin said to have been used by General Crook during his 1872–73 operations. Like most of the Western frontier "forts," the name refers more to its mission than to its architecture. Its principal buildings are constructed around a square that formerly was the parade ground but now is overgrown with shade trees. Other related structures sprawled about the landscape haphazardly.

Citizens had flocked in to the fort for protection. Carr's command had arrived late Wednesday. Thursday morning, while the men were digging a grave at the post cemetery, about six hundred yards east of the main buildings, Indians began to demonstrate. The men hurriedly retired to the fort, along with others working around the perimeter. The Indians soon began firing from two sides. "If we had then had the Gatling gun and 11 pdr. previously invoiced to me they would have been useful," commented Carr, in reporting the action.

First Lieutenant Charles G. Gordon, the post quartermaster, was severely wounded in the leg. As he crumpled to the ground, he commented "I got my billet and my bullet the same day," referring to the fact that with Hentig's death he had come into command of Troop D, 6th Cavalry.[11] Carr's horse was shot from under him. According to Carr:

> The bullets came pretty lively on the north east side at that time and then the Indians gradually circled towards the south. Breastworks were made of rocks, logs, wagons, &c., &c., and the walls of buildings were loopholed. The Indians set on fire some buildings, gardener's houses, and others up the creek, to the

[11] Thomas Cruse, *Apache Days and After*, 132.

N.E. and E. and were approaching the saw mill about 400 yards from the Quarters, when I ordered Capt. [Alexander B.] Mac-Gowan[12] with part of the Company 'D,' 12th Infantry, to retake possession of it, which he did most gallantly and it was thereafter held by him and the civilian Engineer, haycutter and refugees. Towards night the Indians began to give up the contest and some were seen going on the road to the north. Next morning there were but few in sight but some stayed in the vicinity of the Post for several days.

[12] MacGowan, Scottish-born, was brevetted major for his work in this action. Francis B. Heitman, *Historical Register and Dictionary of the United States Army*, I, 666.

III THE RIPPLES SPREAD

As Lieutenant Carter said, Carr must now reopen communications, report his action and its result, put down the uprising, and endeavor to protect the scattered settlers of eastern Arizona and adjacent areas.[1] To do these things, more troops obviously would be needed, and higher authority was eager to send them once the situation was known. In the excitement and uncertainty that followed, however, there occurred the misstep that precipitated the next major incident in the descending whorl of events leading toward the vortex.

Carr sent two civilians, John L. Colvig ("Cibicu Charley," whose slaying a year later initiated the action that concluded with the Battle of Big Dry Wash) and Nat Nobles, the packer, to take word south to Thomas. But they saw Indians and returned to Fort Apache. Carr then dispatched Lieutenant Stanton with thirty-seven men toward Thomas, seventy miles distant. Covering the mountainous portion of the way at night, when Apaches were loath to fight, Stanton reached Thomas the next day with the welcome news that, although Carr and his command had been in a hard fight, most had survived. Colvig, two soldiers, and a civilian, accompanied

[1] Carter, *From Yorktown to Santiago*, 220.

part way by Cooley, who was married to an Apache woman and was trusted by her people, were sent to Fort Wingate, almost two hundred miles to the northeast in New Mexico, with similar reports.

The first thought of military authorities was reinforcements. Rapid action was urged to put down the uprising as quickly as possible. To do this, the army was prepared to smother the area with troops.

Willcox swiftly directed units toward the danger zone. Biddle, in command of operations in southeast Arizona and soon to be placed in command of the new District of the Gila,[2] was ordered from Camp Grant to Camp Thomas and then to Fort Apache. However, unusually high streams, developing from recent heavy rains, hampered his movements.

Troops from Fort Bowie and Fort Huachuca also convened on Thomas for use as indicated by events. Captain Curwen B. McLellan, a veteran of the Victorio campaigns, with Troop L, 6th Cavalry, was sent to old Camp Grant to protect the San Pedro Valley. Captain Adna Romanza Chaffee, with Company I and Company B, Indian Scouts, under Second Lieutenant Francis J. A. Darr, was sent from Fort McDowell toward San Carlos, but was held up at the Wheatfields, about ten miles northwest of the booming mining camp of Globe. He was joined there by Captain Augustus W. Corliss, with two companies of the 8th Infantry, C and F, the latter commanded by Captain Thomas Wilhelm. Chaffee was forced to await pack transportation and then was told to join Lieutenant Colonel William Redwood Price from Fort Verde, commander of the newly created District of the Verde.

2 AT5215AGO1881 McDowell, Presidio, San Francisco, to AG, Washington, September 2, 1881; AT5843AGO1881 Biddle to AAAG, Department of Arizona in the Field, October 13, 1881.

Price left Fort Verde on September 16, reaching Strawberry Valley, below the Mogollon Rim northwest of present-day Payson, that same night. He was accompanied by two veteran scouts, among the best in Arizona at that time, Al Sieber and Dan O'Leary. Sieber was with Darr's company, and O'Leary was with a company of Hualpais Indians raised for this particular task, commanded by First Lieutenant Frederick Von Schrader.

Price's command included the companies of Chaffee, Corliss, and Wilhelm and the two groups of Indian scouts; Captain William M. Wallace, Troop H, and First Lieutenant Henry P. Kingsbury, Troop K, both of the 6th Cavalry; and, from the 12th Infantry, Captain Harry C. Egbert, Company B, Captain John M. Norvell, Company G, and Captain James S. King, Company F. In all he had three troops of cavalry, three companies of infantry, and two companies of Indian scouts.

Heavy rains had made the country a quagmire, almost impassable for wagons. Two of Price's four wagons broke down before he met Chaffee on Tonto Creek, which flows south through the Tonto Basin to join the Salt River at the present Roosevelt Dam. Scouting thoroughly as he marched, Price took his considerable force by way of Pleasant Valley to the Cibecue Valley, where he "found many traces of Cavalry having recently passed over the ground and all traces of Indians obliterated by them." While awaiting suggestions from Fort Apache, he sent Darr's scouts with Sieber twenty-five miles to the north and the Hualpais scouts of Von Schrader, with O'Leary, an equal distance to the south and southeast, to work out Canyon Creek. "These examinations proved to me that the majority of the Indians had moved in a southerly direction, or towards San Carlos, and I so reported," he said.

Price had left Verde on September 16. On the thirtieth he met a courier, about ten miles north of McMillenville, from Colonel Willcox directing him to take over at San Carlos Agency as quickly as possible. He pushed his command throughout the day and by moonlight that night, reaching San Carlos at 7 A.M. on October 1 "after an almost continuous ride of sixty miles," to find that a fresh disaster had struck.[3] Meanwhile, other troop operations were prompted by the Cibecue crisis. Captain Egbert's Company B, 12th Infantry, the garrison outfit at Fort Whipple, was "held in readiness to march to the A and P Railroad to protect working parties," if needed.[4] Captain May H. Stacey of the 12th Infantry was ordered with his company to San Carlos. Willcox sent his aide, First Lieutenant Harry L. Haskell, to the agency also, to "secure alliance of as many as possible" of the Indians. Despite this mustering of his considerable available forces, Willcox called for more reinforcements from California and New Mexico. These were hurriedly sent him,[5] although blunt old General William Tecumseh Sherman, commander in chief of the army, grumbled about the shortage of available forces

[3] Price's lengthy report on all of this and subsequent events at San Carlos is in AT5843AGO1881 Price to AAAG, in the field, October 23, 1881. He was forced to terminate his activities by illness on October 16. He died on December 30. Heitman, *Historical Register and Dictionary of the United States Army*, I, 807.

[4] The Atlantic and Pacific Railroad Company, taken over in 1880 by the Atchison, Topeka and Santa Fe Railway System, reached Holbrook on September 24, and was working westward toward Flagstaff. Its surveying and grading crews were far west of Holbrook, however, and considered to be in danger should hostilities move north. James Marshall, *Santa Fe, the Railroad that Built an Empire*, 168.

[5] Willcox's gathering of his forces, and where he sent them, is summarized in AT5216AGO1881 Willcox to AAG, Military Division of the Pacific, September 2, 1881, before he had definite word of Carr's fate or that of Fort Apache.

and rumors rather than "well authenticated facts."[6] Nevertheless, he growled to McDowell that "I want this annual Apache stampede to end right now, and to effect that result will send every available man in the whole army if necessary."[7] He simply could not envision a situation where soldier-power alone might prove insufficient; in this case it was.

From California a dozen units were hurriedly dispatched to Arizona. There was the 1st Cavalry, Troops C, I, and M, the latter brought all the way from Fort Walla Walla, Washington; the 9th Infantry, Companies B, C, D, F, and K; and Batteries C, L, and H, 4th Artillery.[8] A movement of virtually identical dimensions began from New Mexico. Colonel Luther P. Bradley moved toward Fort Apache from Fort Bayard, near Silver City, with Troops I and K of the 9th Cavalry, Companies F and H of the 13th Infantry, and I of the 16th Infantry. But the big thrust from the east was to be carried out by one of the ablest of all frontier soldiers, Colonel Ranald S. Mackenzie, hurriedly sent into New Mexico from Colorado where, in the "greatest deed of his life," he had forced the Ute Indians, without precipitating a war, to leave their traditional Rocky Mountain homeland for a new reservation in Utah.[9]

With Troops A, B, D, K, I, and L of his 4th Cavalry, Mackenzie hastened to Fort Apache, arriving there on September 25, almost coincidentally with Bradley's command. On his arrival, he was placed by Willcox in command of the District of Apache, succeeding Carr. On October 1, he was ordered by still higher authority to the command "of all

[6] AT5224AGO1881 Sherman to McKeever, September 3, 1881.
[7] AT5488AGO1881 Sherman to McDowell September 16, 1881.
[8] McDowell, *Annual Report*, 1881, *op. cit.*, 137–38.
[9] Ernest Wallace, *Ranald S. Mackenzie on the Texas Frontier*, 187.

troops actively engaged."[10] Both Sherman and Lieutenant General Philip H. Sheridan, then commanding the Military Division of the Missouri, had the greatest confidence in Mackenzie.

Mackenzie was one of the more remarkable officers of the Indian-fighting army. He had a distinguished Civil War record, rising to the brevet rank of major general at twenty-four, although he was not graduated from West Point until June of 1862, and then was appointed to the Corps of Engineers, a branch of the service where promotions, even in wartime, do not ordinarily come with undue rapidity.

Mackenzie was repeatedly wounded, at Second Manassas initially. He rose to command a division of Sheridan's cavalry and to earn the encomium from Grant that he was "the most promising young officer in the Army."[11] He was described by a biographer as a "spare, slim young man of medium height. His youth was accentuated by a clean-shaven face, in a day of heavily-bearded men, except for long sideburns to the curve of his jaws. He had an ascetic, hawk-like face."[12]

Mackenzie, whose career was to be cut short by a tragic and, one might say, almost unnecessary ailment, left no memoirs and virtually no writings of any sort except the terse communications strewn through official files. In these he wasted no words and claimed no laurels. Yet they reveal Mackenzie to have been an extraordinary man and a very able officer. Something of a martinet and exacting of his officers, still Mackenzie rarely chastised one verbally without first citing his good points and afterward explaining to him

[10] AT6209WD1881; 5843AGO1881 Mackenzie to AAG, Department of Arizona, October 15, 1881.

[11] *Dictionary of American Biography*, XII, 95.

[12] Wallace, *Ranald S. Mackenzie on the Texas Frontier*, 10.

in a few words how the failing might best be handled. The record shows that he was equally solicitous of his enlisted men. If even a private was unhappy about some assignment, or a noncommissioned officer displeased that he had been sent to a particular post when he desired to go to another, Mackenzie, upon hearing of it, often took steps to set matters right, to the satisfaction of his soldier.

It is no wonder that, although Mackenzie was sometimes irascible and demanding, often working his men beyond the normal limits of human endurance, his troops frequently demonstrated for him a fierce loyalty no other frontier commander but Crook ever won and few so thoroughly merited.

Mackenzie was a fine combat commander and a tireless campaigner. He construed it to be his mission to rid West Texas of the Indians and to control the Utes in Colorado and the Apaches in New Mexico, and he performed prodigies to do these things. He continued to deserve and to hold the unqualified confidence of Sherman and Sheridan. His one major weakness appeared to be his lack of concern over the fate and interests of the Indians under his control, but in this he differed little from most other officers of that day.[13]

In a message to McDowell, Sherman confidentially said, "If Mackenzie crosses the Mogollons to Fort Apache, I will be forced to give him supreme command of all the troops operating against the Apaches, because of his rank and great vigor. This will not necessarily interfere with Willcox's administrative control of his Department, but will reflect on him and especially on Colonel Carr. . . . I wanted both these officers to strike the Apaches a blow that would inspire at least

[13] *Ibid.* This book, although oriented toward Mackenzie in Texas, presents a summary of his career and an assessment of his character and accomplishments.

Brigadier General George Crook. U.S. Signal Corps Photograph, National Archives.

Colonel Eugene Asa Carr. U.S. Signal Corps Photograph, National Archives.

Colonel Ranald S. Mackenzie. U.S. Signal Corps Photograph, National Archives.

Colonel Orlando Bolivar Willcox. U.S. Signal Corps Photograph, National Archives.

Captain Emmet Crawford. U.S. Signal Corps Photograph, National Archives.

Colonel George A. Forsyth, as he looked in about 1882. In that year he led his troops in a fight against Loco's people, then chased Loco and his band deep into Mexico—without permission from the Mexican government. He was ordered out by Mexican army officers. Arizona Pioneers' Historical Society.

Nana. U.S. Signal Corps Photograph, National Archives.

No photograph ever was taken of Juh, one of the most important Apaches in the Southwest. However, this watercolor of Juh was made by Mrs. Mary P. G. Devereux in January, 1881, at the sub-agency near Camp Thomas. This is its first reproduction in any form. Arizona Pioneers' Historical Society.

Loco. U.S. Signal Corps Photograph, National Archives.

Geronimo. U.S. Signal Corps Photograph, National Archives.

Chatto. U.S. Signal Corps
Photograph, National Ar-
chives.

Chihuahua. U.S. Signal Corps
Photograph, National Ar-
chives.

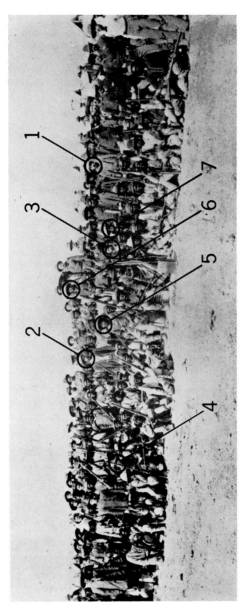

The only photograph ever taken of the Crook expeditionary party that went into the Sierra Madre in 1883 was this one, taken April 22, 1883, at Willcox, Arizona, by Charles S. Baker. Tentatively identified are: 1. Captain John Gregory Bourke, 2. Scout Sam Bowman, 3. Captain Emmet Crawford, 4. Scout Al Sieber, 5. Scout Archie McIntosh, 6. Interpreter Mickey Free, 7. Captain Adna Romanza Chaffee. Arizona Pioneers' Historical Society.

respect, but if Mackenzie gets there he will surely carry things with a high hand."[14] He added, the next day, while correctly anticipating outraged protests from Willcox over the assignment of another officer to a virtually autonomous command within his department, that nevertheless "if General Mackenzie will make an end to Apache wars he may be sure of his reward."[15] But not even Mackenzie could do that.

By this time there were twenty-three military troops, companies, and batteries, in addition to those normally assigned to Arizona, milling about in the southeastern portion of the territory. Their presence no doubt contributed to the more serious outbreak that followed, as John Philip Clum insisted.[16] Or perhaps those Indians about to break out were concerned over possible punishment for past depredations. It may be that they merely were apprehensive of military action against them for undefined offenses.

Meanwhile, however, what of the hostiles from Cibecue?

Leaving aside for the moment the Chiricahua squall making up, let us return to follow the discoveries of army investigators as they studied in detail the Cibecue action and its aftermath, identifying those Indians who had been involved, seeking to learn what had become of the mutinous scouts and other hostiles. In this way it may be possible to see more clearly the connection between the Cibecue incident and subsequent events.

There is an ambiguous passage in Cruse's memoirs sug-

[14] AT5488AGO1881 Sherman to McDowell, September 19, 1881.

[15] AT5508AGO1881 Sherman to McDowell, September 20, 1881.

[16] John Philip Clum, "Apache Misrule," *New Mexico Historical Review*, Vol. V, No. 2 (April, 1930), 140–41; Vol. V, No. 3 (July, 1930), 221–39. In these articles Clum, a former San Carlos agent, passionately argues the case for the Indians from the events at Cibecue through the subsequent Chiricahua outbreak.

gesting, incidentally, that the redoubtable Nana, the wily and aged Warm Springs troublemaker from New Mexico, had been present at that action, though this seems dubious.[17]

Sherman, always impulsive and inclined to sound rather bloodthirsty, said, "I will approve the most severe measures as a punishment for the treachery of the Apaches."[18] He told the adjutant general to inform McDowell that "I expect Willcox to destroy the renegade Apaches; that we dont care about details. . . . I only want to hear results, not intentions"[19] and to tell Sheridan that "every Indian who aided in the attack on Genl Carr's party must be killed or arrested and held for trial . . . there must be no half way measures."[20]

Willcox apparently improved on the most demanding of Sherman's orders, suggesting that Carr, in the latter's words, "hang without trial, prisoners who might be taken."[21] Carr replied that "I am not prepared to hang summarily, the deserting and treacherous scouts. I think it would be well not to hang any, till after all have fully shown their hands, as it would make the rest desperate. . . . If it can be proven

[17] Cruse, *Apache Days and After*, 118. Eve Ball reports that she was told by Ace Daklugie, a son of Juh, that Nana had visited the medicine man, attended at least one "prayer" session, and on a misty pre-dawn personally had seen Noch-ay-del-klinne call up the bodies of the three greatest of their chiefs: Mangas Coloradas, Cochise, and Victorio. "The word of Nana could not be questioned," added her informant. Eve Ball, "Cibicu, an Apache Interpretation," in *Troopers West*, 128.

[18] AT5274AGO1881 Sherman to Drum, September 11, 1881.

[19] AT5361AGO1881 Sherman to AG, Washington, September 10, 1881.

[20] AT5367AGO1881 Sherman to AG, Washington, September 11, 1881.

[21] Carr makes this charge in formal charges and specifications against Willcox, AT1589AGO1883, of which this is specification two to charge three. Willcox and Carr, who apparently detested each other, engaged in a lengthy series of wrangles, which are outside the scope of this work, but from which come occasional glimpses of light on the darker convolutions within the department. This dispute is described in some detail in King, *War Eagle*, 215–32.

that they only deserted, and did not fire on us, there should be a difference in their punishment."[22] This view, as we have seen, later was supported by General McDowell.

More than two months later, Captain Egbert, then at Fort Grant, was ordered to investigate the whole uprising "and if possible segregate the individuals actually concerned," with the help of interpreter Merejildo Grijalva, a trustworthy man of undoubted competence.[23] Egbert wasted no time. He filed his lengthy report within three weeks, summarizing the confusing details of the uprising and naming each of the hostiles and describing his part in the events.[24]

According to Egbert, there was some difference of opinion as to the participation of Indians of Pedro's band in the hostilities. On August 27, just before the affair on Cibecue Creek, Lieutenant Carter and First Lieutenant John Gregory Bourke,[25] of General George Crook's staff, visited Pedro's camp. They found the Apaches

[22] AT1589WD1883 Carr to Willcox from Fort Apache, September 10, 1881.

[23] LS4385DA1881 Benjamin to Egbert November 22, 1881. Merejilda, born at Bacauchi, Sonora, of Opata Indian parents, was captured by the Apaches at the age of ten and held by them for eight years. After his release he was, at various times, an interpreter, scout, and expert on Apaches and their ways. He married a Mexican woman who also had been captured by the Apaches. See the lengthy biographical article by Charles D. Poston, noted Arizona pioneer, in the *Arizona Star*, Tucson, October 3, 1880. Born about 1840, Merejilda died about 1916 at Solomonville. See also Rita Rush, " 'El Chivero'— Merejildo Grijalva," *Arizoniana*, Vol. I, No. 3 (Fall, 1960), 8–9.

[24] AT4675DA1881 Egbert to AAG, Department of Arizona, December 10, 1881. This complete report used briefly here is a most valuable summary of the events during and following the Cibecue outbreak.

[25] Bourke, one of the more attractive and intellectual figures of the Southwestern military frontier, was on detached service from April, 1881, for some time. He pursued ethnological interests among the Navahos, Hopis, and Apaches, which accounts for his presence at the camp of Pedro at this time. George Washington Cullum, *Biographical Register of the Officers and Graduates of the U.S. Military Academy at West Point, N.Y.*, III, 131–32.

full of Indian rum, galloping and running up and down, excited, and irritable; and as Lieut. Carter expressed it, more saucy than he had ever seen the Apaches in eight years experience. They inquired of Lieut. Burke [*sic*] if he had passed the Navajoes on the road to Apache and stated they expected that tribe to visit them at that time. Both these officers considered the probability of an early outbreak of this band imminent from their conduct.

Tiffany, Egbert stated, thought Pedro's band deeply implicated in the Cibecue affair; Carr rejected that belief. Continuing his description of the uprising, Egbert stated that at dawn, following the attack on the military, and after the soldiers had pulled out for Apache, the Indians ransacked the camp ground,

> collected into a heap a quantity of flour, canned stuff, &c., also saddles, aparejos [the pack saddles of that day] and other equipment of a [pack] train. These they set on fire and then dug up the bodies, the dead, mutilating that of Capt. Hentig. Some of them, including nine scouts, then started for Fort Apache where they were present during the attack on that post, while 21 went rapidly west to Pleasant Valley on Cherry Creek. This party had representatives from five bands of Cibecue and Carrizo Creek [Apaches, who were] White Mountain Indians, [including] four from the band of Sanchez.

Egbert names these Indians and gives their bands and leaders, most of them forgotten today. They included Na-ti-o-tish, whose name should be remembered, for we shall hear more of him, and his co-leader, Ne-big-ja-gy, and seven members of their band. Ne-big-ja-gy was a brother of Noch-ay-del-klinne, the slain medicine man. This is the band that struck the Middleton Ranch, killing two men, wounding another, and running off about seventy-five head of horses. While most of the twenty-one depredating Indians gathered the stock and ran it off, Na-ti-o-tish and Ne-big-ja-gy and three other Indians carried out the assault on the house. The stock was driven east to Cedar Creek, on the White Mountain Reservation.

Egbert also reported that during these turbulent days there were five bands from the San Carlos area at Fort Apache, in addition to Pedro's band, which habitually resided within its environs. These included "Bonito's band, consisting of himself and four other Chiricahuas Indians, and, 2nd, George's [band], containing about 26 White Mountain Indians. Both these bands had overstayed their passes [from San Carlos] and were therefore absent without leave."

On the morning of August 31, the day after Carr's fight and before the assault on Fort Apache, Indians killed a courier en route to Camp Thomas, three other soldiers, three Mormons (all six on "7-Mile Hill," about eight miles south of Fort Apache), and another civilian at a ranch on Turkey Creek, where they also stole some stock.

"The Indians who committed these murders," reported Egbert, "were 1st Bonito and his small Chiricahua band of four men ... 2nd, George's band of White Mountain Indians numbering 26 [whom he named] ... , 3rd, small bands of outlaws [whom he also named, including Mosby and Gar, two noted turbulent spirits] ... , 4th, Pedro's band (in part). ..." Included among the seven Indians of Pedro's band were the well-known Apaches Al-che-say (Alchise) and U-clen-ny. Egbert added that "U-clen-ny and Bonito each claimed to have killed one man."

"After these murders ... at 8:30 next morning September 1, [the Indians] came to one of Pedro's camps about 2 miles from Fort Apache. Here, after a long talk they separated, some going north about 18 or 20, and 32 remaining.

"About 2 P.M. fire was commenced on the post from the opposite direction in the trees when the 32 charged towards the post, dismounted and also opened fire. . . . The firing was kept up with no effect upon the post for some time, when the Indians withdrew."

He said the "parties concerned in the attack on Fort Apache were George's band, the small band of renegades under Mosby, nine of the scouts . . . and most probably the majority of Pedro's band.

"The most prominent Indians in the attack on Colonel Carr's command, besides the scouts, were Sanchez, [four others], Ne-big-ja-gy and Na-ti-o-tish."

The captain noted the difficulty in successfully prosecuting any of the Indians in the courts "unless Indian testimony can be received," which was unlikely. He recommended that the leaders, when all were caught, be confined on the Dry Tortugas, an island group off Florida where there had once been a Civil War prison camp, or some similar place, and others be removed to the Indian Territory. "This would break the prominence of the White Mountain tribe . . . and be a most salutary warning to the remaining tribes," he believed.

"The number of the hostiles must always remain uncertain. The agent on September 3, reported 220 out, as far as he could ascertain and not over 260, but in this number he included the whole of Pedro's band, part of which remained near Cooley's Ranch 30 miles from Fort Apache and was not in the attack on the post, also some small bands, some of the members of which are known to have remained quietly at their corn fields."

"Pedro's band, discouraged by the result of the attack on Apache and probably persuaded by the ranchman, Cooley, remained at his place," said Egbert. After the fighting, the hostiles scattered, "some back to the Cibicu ranches [rancherias] and in Pedro's camp near Apache, while those who like George belonged to the Agency [San Carlos] or Sub Agency [near Camp Thomas] took refuge in the camps of the friendly Indians at those points." About sixty warriors, "after long and anxious consultation," determined to surrender and did so about September 20. But about forty of the most intransigent hostiles, including Na-ti-o-tish, remained out, hiding quietly for almost a year.[26] Na-ti-o-tish was reported slain in late November, 1881, but the rumor was premature.[27]

Scarcely had the fighting abated when the hostiles, worried over white retaliation, held long conferences among themselves. Most decided that their best course would be surrender. Sanchez, one of the Apaches most prominently identified by whites at Cibecue, four other leaders, and the bands of all of them gave up unconditionally on September 21 at San Carlos. It was the firm intention to try them and punish them, if suitable charges could be agreed upon.[28] On September 25, Tiffany reported to the commissioner of Indian affairs on the surrenders:

> I informed the five chiefs said to be hostile that they would have to surrender themselves, men, arms and ammunition to the military. They said they would do as they had agreed to do with me, that I could kill them if I wanted to. . . . I then turned them over to Lt. Haskell who asked how many of their bucks were in with them. They told him about 60 and requested confirmation of chief of scouts [Al Sieber] who had counted them, who confirmed the statement.

26 LS1739DA1882 Willcox to AG, Washington, May 30, 1882.

27 AT6671AGO1881 Chaffee to AAG, Department of Arizona, November 28, 1881.

28 LS3551DA1881 Benjamin to Price, September 22, 1881.

Complications arose, however, when the five leaders were confined, and their sixty followers, camped about six miles up the San Carlos River from the agency, became excited and evaporated into the wilderness. Meanwhile, the bands of George and Bonito were bivouacked near the subagency, at Camp Thomas. The agent, Ezra Hoag, thought they could be picked up by the military with little trouble. Tiffany, eager to contact the three-score breakaways and talk them once more into coming in, urged the officers to postpone any action against George and Bonito until he could succeed in his delicate task. Willcox agreed. "I am informed they are coming in," Tiffany reported, "and without in any way wishing to interfere or reflect upon the military I believe with a little patience and prudence this whole matter can be settled."

Haskell, during this period, had gone to the subagency and talked with Hoag, George, and Bonito. The Indians said they would not surrender to military field commanders, but would go with Hoag to the subagency and surrender to Willcox, who was there in person. On the way in, however, George was thrown from his horse and injured. Bonito went on in and surrendered to Willcox.

"I hope the military will . . . punish them according to the degree in which they have participated, thus giving to them and all Indians a salutary warning and bringing this outbreak which has been somewhat exaggerated to a speedy conclusion," said Tiffany.[29] Nevertheless, George and Bonito were paroled for the time being.

By mid-January Willcox reported that seventy Indians were being held for suspected complicity in the uprising, of whom three were scouts. Forty-one were at Fort Lowell, near

[29] This detailed summary is contained in AT5843AGO1881 Tiffany to Indian Commissioner, September 25, 1881.

Tucson, twenty-six were at Camp Thomas, and the three scouts were at Fort Grant.[30] Willcox already had asked instructions of higher authority at San Francisco in view of the fact that evidence against many of the prisoners was flimsy, or otherwise not suitable for court use.[31] Late in February the secretary of war ordered the release of all of them except the mutinous scouts; all three were hanged in March.[32]

The forty recalcitrants who had never come in remained, however, arrogant and hostile, biding their time in the recesses of the mammoth reservations. They would be heard from again.

[30] AT232AGO1882 Willcox to AG, Washington, January 19, 1882.

[31] AT73DA1882 Willcox to AAG, Division of the Pacific, Presidio, San Francisco, January 11, 1882.

[32] AT469DA1882 Benjamin to C.O., Camp Thomas, February 28, 1882.

IV THE CHIRICAHUAS BOLT

The precise reasons for the flight of some of the Chiricahua
Indians from San Carlos to Old Mexico, the next step in the
worsening situation in the Southwest, are not clear, even at
this date. The military was urged not to attempt to arrest the
White Mountain band of twenty-six hostiles under George or
the five-man band of the Chiricahua, Bonito, on ration-issue
day because of the confusion it might create among the excitable Apaches. But this was attempted, nonetheless, possibly because the Indians were more "available" on that day
than any other. It may be that insufficient force was mustered
for the effort, or that the Indians were flushed into the hills
by the sight of as many troops as were gathered, or perhaps
their own premonitions of punishment for past depredations
were a factor.

It has been charged that corruption on the reservation had
led to the denial of rations and other supplies to many Indians, and that this caused intense dissatisfaction.[1] It would
seem unlikely that this could have been the immediate cause
for the *émeute*, however, because even the most corrupt officials saw to it that the chiefs and headmen were well fed,[2]

[1] Lockwood, *The Apache Indians*, 244.

and in this case the flight was directed by the normal leaders of the bands.

There may have been more elusive causes. Certainly the combative, volatile nature of those Chiricahuas who followed Juh, Nachez, and Geronimo, cannot be ignored. It is conceivable that these Indians were ready for a break in any event and took the abortive arrest attempt as an excuse.

At any rate, the explosion occurred.

The action that apparently precipitated it was an attempt to terminate the paroles of Bonito and George and to take them into custody. Then, on October 1, Carr, at San Carlos, received a terse message: "Hoag at sub agency reports that George and Bonito left with their bands last night, probably towards old home and that Chiricahuas broke and went south. You will at once use your command in the most vigorous pursuit."[3]

Major George B. Sanford, of the 1st Cavalry, and Major Biddle, of the 6th, had been ordered "with sufficient forces to capture the hostiles" (George and Bonito and their people), near whom were camped some mercurial Chiricahuas under Nachez, a son of Cochise, and Juh, a noted war leader whose band most likely had killed the celebrated Lieutenant Howard B. Cushing a decade before.[4] The Chiricahuas, Willcox later reported, had been "ready to break."[5]

Willcox said that Tiffany's apparent scheme had been to treat the hostiles "kindly" until all had come in and then

[2] See Dan L. Thrapp, *Al Sieber, Chief of Scouts*, 290–92, for an example of how corruption sometimes came about and the precautions used when it did.

[3] AT1589WD1883, included in the list of charges preferred by Carr against Willcox.

[4] Thrapp, *Conquest of Apacheria*, 72–77.

[5] LS4244DA1881 Willcox to AAG, Military Division of the Pacific, December 12, 1881.

seize them. He regarded such a method as "treacherous" and said that "my plan was for the Indians to surrender unconditionally or be treated as public enemies." This intention, he said, was communicated to Lieutenant Haskell, to Sanford, and to Biddle, while Tiffany's views seemingly had been sent to Hoag, in charge at the subagency.

Sanford, Willcox continued, "executed his orders successfully and took forty-seven prisoners, all male warriors," while Biddle "brought in nineteen squaws from the Coyotero [the White Mountain Apaches] and Chiricahua camps." But because the operation was not a clean sweep, disaster resulted. George and his band of White Mountain–Coyotero Apaches slipped away, back into the wilderness of the reservation hinterlands, later to be arrested.

The Chiricahuas, however, including Bonito and his tiny group of four hostiles, Nachez, Juh, and, probably, Geronimo (who was not then important enough as a war leader to be specifically named in dispatches), about seventy warriors in all, "broke out on the warpath . . . whether in consequence of this movement, or of Major Biddle's manner of proceeding, or whether the Chiricahuas apprehended being disarmed, concerning which they had heard reports and shown much anxiety, or whether they intended to quit the reservation anyhow, is not known. That some of them went on compulsion of their chiefs is known."[6]

Juh and his band had come in from Mexico and voluntarily surrendered in January, 1880, but their volatile history had begun long before. Juh had fled into Mexico in 1876, when some of the Chiricahuas were moved from their old reservation to San Carlos. Geronimo and others fled San Carlos in April, 1878, to rejoin Juh in Mexico. Haskell, Thomas Jef-

[6] *Ibid.*

fords, who knew the Chiricahuas well and was trusted by them, and Archie McIntosh, a well-known scout, made contact with the hostile band in Mexico late in 1879, and talked them into coming back. They did, locating themselves near the subagency.[7]

Carr grumbled that "I think the great mistake that has been made was by . . . Willcox, in having brought the band of Chiricahuas under Whoo [Juh] out of Mexico. They came or were brought out almost conquerors, not as captives." He added that even the Mexicans had objected to "giving these red-handed murderers an asylum in the United States."[8] But that had been done and now was to be undone.

While Mackenzie was placed in command of active operations in the area, Willcox retained his administrative command and nominal control over the department. This led to an inevitable confusion of orders sent to the various field commanders, particularly because communications between Willcox and Mackenzie were intermittent, when they existed at all. For example, Carr was ordered to make a "vigorous pursuit" of the fleeing Indians by Willcox and about the same time was ordered by Mackenzie to take charge of San Carlos.[9]

"Telegraphic communication with Colonel Mackenzie being cut off for the moment," Willcox later said, "I ordered two companies 6th Cavalry under Lieut. [Gilbert E.] Overton, out from Camp Thomas on the trail, and two companies of the 1st Cavy under Sanford" also to pursue the Chiricahuas. Sanford, almost simultaneously, was ordered by Mackenzie to take charge of the "pursuit of the Chiricahuas

[7] Ralph Hedrick Ogle, *Federal Control of the Western Apaches 1848–1886*, 198–99n.

[8] AT970AGO1883 Carr to Sherman April 6, 1882.

[9] LS4244DA1881 Willcox to AAG, Military Division of the Pacific, December 12, 1881.

JUH'S ROUTE FROM FORT THOMAS TO FORT GRANT

and matters in southern Arizona," the two orders fortunately coinciding in this case.[10] Price, now under Carr's command, urged the colonel "that I be sent through Aravaipa Canyon in pursuit of them," confident he could cut their trail. His request was turned down for reasons not entirely clear.[11] The hostiles, however, did not go south by that route. It was the veteran Indian fighter, Captain Reuben F. Bernard, commanding Company G, 1st Cavalry, who struck the enemy. He was in effective command of the 1st Cavalry units because Major Sanford was ill of malaria, an old ailment.[12]

The two companies of the 1st Cavalry and two of the 6th moved rapidly down the trail of the fleeing Apaches toward Cedar Springs, between Camp Thomas and Fort Grant, but the Indians reached there first with murderous results. They killed the telegraph operator, a man named Gidell, and four soldiers engaged in repair work on the line. Their quick eyes saw a freight wagon train approaching Cedar Springs and, one mile east of the place, they attacked and overwhelmed it. They killed Bartolo Samaniego, its leader, "a fine young Mexican," who had been in charge of the transportation of the 6th Cavalry regiment from Santa Fe to Tucson six years earlier and was well known to veterans of that outfit.[13] They also slew five teamsters. "Six mules were killed, hitched to the wagon. The flour sacks were cut and the flour scattered around the wagon. Samaniego and his men made a stubborn fight for their lives," said a news report.[14]

[10] AT5843AGO1883 Mackenzie to AAG, Department of Arizona, October 15, 1881. Same serial number, Sanford to AAAG, Willcox, October 18, 1881.
[11] LS4244DA1881 op. cit.
[12] AT5843AGO1881, Sanford endorsement to Bernard's report to AAG, Department of Arizona, October 14, 1881.
[13] Carter, From Yorktown to Santiago, 224.
[14] Arizona Star, October 7, 1881. The casualties are identified by name in

But the Indians dallied too long in the vicinity, and the soldiers caught up with them.

"Upon arriving at Cedar Springs . . . it was reported that Indians were in the vicinity and had captured a freight train and killed the teamsters," said Captain Bernard, in his report of the action. The broad trail was followed, although it was late in the day, by the troopers of the 1st and 6th Cavalry outfits.

A steady trot was taken up. As the indians were going towards Grant, where Lt. Overton's family was, he became very anxious and asked permission to go ahead at a quicker gait; this being granted, Overton's Battalion had just got in the advance, and was moving at a gallop, when they came on some dead men. Slackening his gait to see who the dead men were, the indians opened fire from Overton's front and left, the indians being in a strong place in the rocks and timber. Overton at once dismounted and moved his Battalion towards the indians' position.

I at once deployed my company to the left, mounted, moving well to the left, driving the indians from a hill, then moved to the right front into line as skirmishers, which brought Overton's Battalion on my right, when all advanced driving the indians well into the mountains. It was now getting dark, and the indians having a very strong position in Mount Graham, I established the skirmish line in as strong a position as I could get, and held it, though the indians kept up a heavy fire, until about nine o'clock at night.

About eight at night, the indians made a charge on the left of the line coming within a few yards of it [other sources say within ten feet of their enemy]. A heavy fire was kept up for a

---

Carr's charges against Willcox, specification eight to charge one, AT1589AGO-1883, *op. cit.* In specifications one through three to charge four of this document Carr accuses Willcox personally of dodging this fight "in a cowardly and shameful manner."

few minutes, when the indians withdrew, giving that flank no more trouble during the engagement. . . . The indians got away by going high up on the mountain and passing by and about two miles from, our right flank. . . . I withdrew the Battalion about half past nine o'clock, and moved to Fort Grant, where we arrived about midnight.[15]

Reinforcements had arrived from Grant, but too late to be useful.[16] Bernard's losses were a sergeant killed, three men wounded, and fifteen horses killed or wounded.

There are several interesting features of this fight, as reported by Bernard. One is that this is a rare occasion on which the Apaches fought after dark, although aided in this case by a bright moon. Their reluctance to fight at night is a well-established fact, but its reasons are obscure, although their belief in, and fear of, ghosts may be involved.[17] The fact of the Indian "charge" also is unusual. It indicates more discipline than usually was evident among the Apaches, and it is a tribute to Juh's leadership. So, too, were the Indians' well-conducted withdrawal procedures. According to one authority, they methodically slit the throats of their dogs, which might have made noises giving their movements away, and their light-colored horses, which could have been observed in the gloom, and sped south, picking up $20,000 to $30,000 worth of horses from ranchers on their way.[18] Obviously their leader exhibited considerable competence.

[15] AT5843AGO1881 Bernard to AAG, Department of Arizona, October 14, 1881.

[16] McDowell, *Annual Report*, 1881, 146.

[17] Morris E. Opler, *An Apache Life-Way*, 229–37, discusses this fear, along with "darkness sickness" and allied beliefs.

[18] Will C. Barnes, *Arizona Place Names*, 1st ed., 84–85. AT1589AGO1883, specification eight to charge one, Carr *vs.* Willcox. Another indication that Juh knew the value of discipline and, virtually alone among the great Apache

Juh hurried his people southward, toward Sonora, managing to avoid further significant contact with the soldiers, although the region was scoured by troops. Captain Henry Wagner, 1st Cavalry, took Companies C and M, with Von Schrader's Hualpais scouts and Dan O'Leary, south along the eastern face of the Chiricahua uplift as far as Silver Creek and San Bernardino, on the line, without striking fresh sign, although his scouts found the trails of Bernard, several days old, and the Indians going south, also too old for any hope of contact.[19] Captain Curwen B. McLellan of the 6th Cavalry was ordered to scout down the western slope of the Chiricahuas. He also failed to find the Indians, although he met Wagner near San Bernardino.[20] Bernard moved rapidly south on the actual trail of the hostiles, following it the length of the Dragoon Mountains, directly south of Fort Grant.

Bernard had left Willcox Station, on the Southern Pacific, early on October 4, following sign. During the day the column overtook Captain Henry Carroll, with Companies F and H of the 9th Cavalry from New Mexico. "The whole force took up the gallop, over the rough and rocky hills, skirmishing with the Indians, until they were driven into a very strong position in the mountains, near the South Pass," below the Dragoons. The troops were placed, just before dark, in a semicircle around the mountain position. Nevertheless, at

---

leaders, exacted it from his followers, was in his probable fight with Howard Cushing. In this sharp engagement the surviving noncommissioned officer remarked on the decided and effective control the Indian leader had over his warriors—a most novel quality among Apache fighting men. See Thrapp, *Conquest of Apacheria*, 76–77.

[19] AT5843AGO1883 Wagner to AAG, Department of Arizona, October 15, 1881.

[20] AT5843AGO1883 Sanford to AAAG, Willcox, October 18, 1881.

dawn it was discovered that the hostiles had slipped out westward, into the San Pedro Valley, then turned south within six or eight miles of Tombstone, then east through Mule Pass, crossed the Sulphur Springs Valley and climbed into the southern end of the Chiricahuas, crossed the San Bernardino plains into and through the Guadalupe Mountains and so swept blithely into sunlit Old Mexico, safe from further harassment.[21]

"This pursuit was conducted through heavy rains, which caused the Indians to abandon many horses and mules, and much plunder, but as they were able to change horses, it was impossible for troops to overtake them," Carter wrote.[22]

Sanford, denying reports that Bernard had dallied two days at Soldiers Holes, a watering place at the south end of the Chiricahuas, twenty-five miles north of the line, said Bernard's forces "have made a march and pursuit almost unexampled in Indian warfare."[23]

Regardless of the vigor of the pursuit, however, the Southwest now could gird itself for fresh hostilities, for the Chiricahuas in the Sierra Madre were beyond pursuit. It was apparent they would never rest until they had been joined by their people still on the San Carlos Reservation and had shown their inveterate hostility and contempt for the soldier guardians of the border states, as well as their thirst for booty from north of the line.

[21] AT5843AGO1883 Bernard to AAG, Department of Arizona, October 14, 1881.

[22] Carter, *From Yorktown to Santiago*, 226–27.

[23] AT5843AGO1883 Sanford to AAAG, Willcox, supplemental report, October 20, 1881.

V AN UNEASY INTERLUDE

Now that the hostile Chiricahuas had reached Old Mexico, Colonel Mackenzie was relieved from command of field forces in southeastern Arizona, to the gratification, no doubt, of both himself and Willcox. He left Fort Thomas on October 17 for New Mexico. There, almost immediately, he was named to command the district, in succession to Hatch.[1] He reported that his six 4th Cavalry troops reached New Mexico "in a very unserviceable condition," with only about thirty effectives in each, while the duty they faced "promises to be such as to require these companies to be in the most thoroughly effective condition. . . . The situation in Southern New Mexico is more dangerous than at any previous time for years" with the hostiles "expected to commence depredations on our border on a very extensive scale."[2]

Not only the United States forces but those of Mexico as well were actively concerned with the Apaches. Every commanding officer north of the border—Hatch, Mackenzie, Willcox, and, later, Crook—realized that the border must

[1] LS445DNM1881 Loud to Baker, October 30, 1881.
[2] LS451DNM1881 Mackenzie to AAG, Fort Leavenworth, November 1, 1881.

not be a barrier to effective pursuit and studied the possibility of striking the hostiles south of it when feasible.

Field commanders continually urged that some agreement relating to pursuit south of the border be reached with Mexican authorities. Although negotiations and discussions toward that end were from time to time carried out, the border remained largely sealed to troops until July 29, 1882, when an agreement at last was reached and signed at Washington.[3] The agreement, in its essential parts, provided that "the regular federal troops of the two Republics may reciprocally cross the boundary line of the two countries, when they are in close pursuit of a band of savage Indians." It said that such crossings "shall only occur in the unpopulated or desert parts of said boundary line," which were defined as those areas "at least two leagues distant from any encampment or town of either country."

The agreement said further that "the Commander of the troops which cross the frontier in pursuit of Indians, shall, at the time of crossing or before if possible, give notice of his march to the nearest military commander or civil authority of the country whose territory he enters," and further that "the pursuing force shall retire to its own territory as soon as it shall have fought the band of which it is in pursuit or have lost its trail. In no case shall the forces of the two countries . . . remain in the foreign territory for any time longer than is necessary to make the pursuit of the band whose trail they follow."

[3] *Agreement between the United States and Mexico establishing the reciprocal right to pursue savage Indians across the boundary line; concluded, signed, and exchanged at Washington July 29, 1882. United States Statutes at Large*, XXII, 934–36. This agreement was modified, with regard to its time limit, September 21, 1882, *Statutes at Large*, XXII, 939; June 28, 1883, *Statutes at Large*, XXIII, 734–35; October 31, 1884, *Statutes at Large*, XXIII, 806–807.

The initial agreement was to remain in force for two years, but could be terminated by four months' notice by either government. It was extended, however, from 1882 through the Geronimo troubles which ended in late 1886.

Lack of a formal agreement had not prevented border violations from time to time. These violations were due, probably, to young officers who were unable to resist the temptation to continue across the unguarded frontier when they were following interesting sign. For example, early in November, 1881, First Lieutenant Thomas Garvey of the 1st Cavalry and his "small detachment of soldiers and Indian guides" slipped into Sonora. They were caught, causing Willcox to formally assure General José Tiburcio, commander in chief of the Army of Sonora, that the matter would be properly investigated, although not saying that Garvey would be punished.[4] Somewhat more serious was the penetration into Chihuahua of First Lieutenant David N. McDonald of the 4th Cavalry in January, 1882. In command of a company of scouts, this brave and vigorous officer crossed the line toward Lake Guzman, then went westerly, reaching the settlement of Asuncion, fifty-five miles southwest of present-day Columbus, New Mexico, where he was arrested by Mexican authorities. Mackenzie messaged General Carlos Fuero, commanding the Second Military District from Chihuahua, that McDonald's miniature invasion was made "without the knowledge or authority of myself or any superior officer." He thanked Fuero for releasing McDonald and said he would investigate the matter, adding that he had warned all officers against crossing the line "unless close in pursuit of marauding Indians," which McDonald obviously was not.[5]

[4] LS4558DA1881 Willcox to Tiburcio, Guaymas, December 12, 1881.
[5] LS55DNM1882 Mackenzie to Fuero, January 21, 1882.

Mackenzie realized that too impetuous action by junior officers might cause repercussions. He therefore told Lieutenant Colonel George Forsyth, commanding troops in southern New Mexico, that he considered it "unwise to leave any discretion to officers about crossing the Mexican boundary line." He then directed Forsyth to "instruct officers in charge of scouting parties not to cross that line under any circumstances."[6] Forsyth no doubt passed along Mackenzie's order. Nevertheless, he was to be involved in the largest of all technical border violations within a very few months.

Forsyth, a pivotal figure in certain Apache actions to follow, remains something of an enigma, although he was a bluff and open soldier. Once beleaguered on Beecher's Island on the north fork of the Republican River in September of 1868 by superior numbers of Cheyennes, it is probable that he learned the perils of fighting Indians with forces inferior in size. He had been brevetted brigadier general for that action, getting out of it by the skin of his teeth, badly wounded. It is possible that such a fright was thrown into him then that it carried over and affected his operations against the Apaches. At least it would seem so from the record.

Reports from Mexico, meanwhile, were not clear, though they indicated that the Apaches were operating in their normal manner in that country and that Mexican forces were occasionally effective against them. Thus, Captain Theodore A. Baldwin of the 10th Cavalry messaged the post adjutant at Camp Davis, Texas, from the Presidio on the Río Grande in late November, 1881, that "the commanding officer of the Mexican forces at and near Del Norte [reported that] he surrounded and captured forty-four (44) Indians of the San Carlos reservation . . . and that there were but sixteen (16)

6 LS54DNM1882 Dorst to C.O., Fort Cummings, January 21, 1882.

more who were out hunting at the time, 3 of which had returned and been taken" and he expected to get the others.[7] Some Apaches may have been captured, but it is likely that they were errant Mescaleros rather than Apaches from San Carlos, none of whose fugitives is known to have wandered nearly so far east.

Late in the year Willcox messaged his superiors his assessment of the situation, which he found fluid, to say the least.

There are not troops enough in the Dept. to meet emergencies, now that Juh and Nachise [Nachez] are out, but the emergency may not arise before Spring. I have lost no time seeking the co-operation of the Mexican military, who I find full of professions, but shy of making any practical agreement for attacking the renegade Indians. They are very sensitive about our crossing the border, and I think they feel sore because we do nothing to prevent Cow-Boy raids [against them]. I am in correspondence also with Mackenzie, with mutual agreement for co-operation. He says he thinks there is no use stationing troops on the border or attempting to catch the Indians by pursuit, but the only successful way is to make war upon them where they live, and have their families and property, which is all true, if they did not live in Mexico....

I have sent spies into Chihuahua, and have one in that state now [he was captured by Mexican civil authorities in Chihuahua in February];[8] the last information was that [Colonel Joaquin] Terrazas was not molesting the Chiricahuas, but intended to surprise and kill them after they are settled. . . . I have a no. of reports of small parties of five or ten hostiles coming into Arizona, but the border has been patrolled by troops of [Fort] Huachuca and [Fort] Bowie.[9]

[7] AT6703AGO1881 Baldwin to Post Adjutant, Fort Davis, November 26, 1881.
[8] LS386DA1882 Willcox to Mackenzie, February 20, 1882.

It was the determination of the wild Apaches now in Mexico to retain their contacts with friends on the San Carlos Reservation, and ultimately to lure them away, that was to create the major difficulty in the days to come. These apparent contacts from south of the border continued, as we shall see.

The clamor, meanwhile, from the citizenry of Arizona and New Mexico mounted. Cries in the press and elsewhere had always been heard to "disarm" the Apaches, to remove them from the Southwest so the whites could live at peace there, or at least to shove them farther from the border, so that *émeutes* would be less likely, or not so frequently successful. These cries had reached a peak by late 1881. On January 11, 1882, Secretary of the Interior Samuel Jordan Kirkwood called on brevet Brigadier General Charles Henry Howard to study the situation on the spot and make recommendations. He was the brother of General Oliver Otis Howard who, a decade before, had reached an agreement with Cochise, taking that chief off the warpath, at least in this country.

Like his brother, General Charles Howard was a deeply religious man. He had been editor-in-chief of the Chicago *Advance*, a Congregational newspaper founded in 1867. He had also served as an inspector for the Freedmen's Bureau, the post-Civil War federal agency to aid and protect newly freed Negroes in the South.

Howard was appointed a United States Indian inspector and directed to go to the Mescalero and San Carlos reservations for the purpose of special inquiry. He was to report on the character of their lands, the attitude of the Indians with regard to possible removal to areas "more remote from the

[9] LS4632DA1881 Willcox to AG, Military Division of the Pacific, December 12, 1881.

Mexican border," and on "the condition, feeling and prospect of the Indians."[10] On March 25, he mailed his report concerning San Carlos from that agency. It was a voluminous document and fully detailed.[11]

Howard reported that "only one tribe has any disposition favoring a removal, namely those known as the Warm-Spring Indians," the New Mexico people of whom Victorio and Mangas Coloradas were the most famous leaders. They were so closely related to the Chiricahuas as to be virtually the same people. They warred, raided, and plundered with the Chiricahuas throughout the history of the Southwest, visiting freely back and forth. Both are members of the Gileños group, within the larger Chiricahua–Mescalero division.[12]

Howard noted that the Warm Springs Apaches "have some relatives among the Navajos. The latter have signified a willingness to have them come to live on their Reservation in New Mexico. . . . The tribe here seem to be quite unanimous in their desire to go to the Navajos." He recommended removal under the supervision of Indian Scouts, not soldiers, but it was never undertaken. Throughout the history of the Southwest one catches glimpses of the consanguinity between Navaho and Apache, even though this rarely if ever led to war co-operation, at least after the Spanish period. Howard conceded that even if the Warm Springs were removed to the Navaho Reservation, some of the young men no doubt would run away to join the hostiles.

He said he could "find no good reason" for the removal of

10 Richard S. Maxwell, assistant director, Social and Economic Records Division, National Archives and Records Service, to author, October 3, 1968.

11 LR1849-10-7 Selected Document relating to C. H. Howard, File No. 829, 1882, Howard to Kirkwood, March 25, 1882.

12 John R. Swanton, *The Indian Tribes of North America*, B.A.E. *Bulletin 145*, 329.

the remaining Apache bands or other Indians of San Carlos, and he was sure that "any attempted removal would result in war."

Howard did not think the Indians were too close to the border. He said if they could be caught making for Mexico anywhere, they could be apprehended in the two hundred miles between San Carlos and the border, because the geography was so open and interception therefore very possible—this in spite of the fact that no fleeing party of Apaches ever had been caught making the effort. The inspector urged that the State, Treasury, War, and Interior Departments combine their resources to seal the border, because each department had an interest in the matter: the State Department for diplomatic reasons, the Treasury to prevent smuggling, War for military reasons, and Interior because the Indians were its wards. He suggested a better system of frontier forts. Then Howard turned to the touchiest of all issues, that of disarming the Indians.

> The only [justifiable] reason for their retaining arms (and almost every Indian has his breech-loading rifle), is for the purposes of hunting. But as they have a good issue of fresh beef every week, they do not need the game. . . . I would suggest that the Agent keep the Rifles, and loan them, at his discretion, to anyone who desires to go hunting, and that he give him a pass, to that effect, at the same time, for a limited period, and that both pass and rifle be required to be returned at fixed date.

He conceded that "there will be difficulty in enforcing the relinquishment of arms," but he thought they could be "purchased" by exchange of a cow for each one. He also admitted that "there is a difficulty in the sale of arms to Indians. But if the Indians are allowed to have their rifles when they wish to go out to hunt, it will tend to prevent their purchase of others."

In all of this, Howard reflected common arguments circulating at the time. He was not only overly sanguine, but unrealistic, as well. There were sound arguments for the Indians to retain their arms, aside from their understandable desire to hunt, a pursuit inextricably interlocked with their rich culture. Brigadier General George Crook answered these arguments most cogently in his *Annual Report* for 1883 which, although dated somewhat later, is apropos here.

> The disarming of Indians is very generally believed to be the first step in solving the Indian problem, and it is often insisted on as the one condition precedent to placing them on reservations. In my judgment this is an error.
>
> In the first place it is impossible to disarm Indians. Individuals may be taken in certain instances at such disadvantage as to make it possible to get their arms, but with whole bands or tribes this is hardly possible. I knew that the Chiricahuas had an abundance of the best arms, and yet when they came into our camp, thinking very likely that I would demand the surrender of their arms, many of them were armed only with lances, and others with very indifferent guns, which would have been given up had I demanded them. The result would have been, they would have considered that we were afraid of them, their arms would have still been in their possession, and we would have lost their confidence, which can only be secured by showing them that at their best we have no fear of them. . . .
>
> Neither is it possible to prevent Indians from obtaining arms and ammunition; in this country, money will buy anything. One strong incentive for Indians to go upon the warpath, is to obtain munitions of war, or the means to purchase them. . . .
>
> There is another reason: the Indian knows better than any one else, how necessary arms are for his protection. He has dis-

covered that the Government does not prevent the disreputable class of white men with which he is surrounded from committing depredations upon his reservation, or punish them for their acts. He concludes that he must protect himself.

Deprive the Apache Indians of their arms, and in a short time there would not be a hoof of stock on the reservation.[13]

In his report, Howard also spoke warmly of Judge Aaron H. Hackney, editor of the Globe *Silver Belt,* suggesting that he be given a position of prominence in investigating matters concerning certain Apache prisoners at San Carlos. According to Crook, however, Hackney was a member of a corrupt and infamous "ring" which also included Tiffany and which may well have been a factor in driving the Chiricahuas and their allies from the San Carlos Reservation.[14] The existence of this "ring," and its machinations if it did exist, has never been objectively proved, or even studied, but the contemporary evidence that it did exist, and documentation to that conclusion, is persuasive.

[13] George Crook, *Annual Report,* 1883, 14–15. This report is in the Rutherford B. Hayes Memorial Library of Fremont, Ohio. The Hayes Memorial Library has a large collection of Crook papers to which its director, Watt P. Marchman, has generously given me access. Hereafter cited as Hayes Collection.

[14] See Agent P. P. Wilcox to Interior Secretary H. M. Teller, printed textually in *Arizona Star,* March 13, 1883; Crook to Teller, textually, *Arizona Star,* March 13, 1883; Crook to Teller, March 27, 1883, Hayes Collection, particularly the postscript.

VI THE HOSTILES SLIP NORTH

One obvious necessity for military commanders was precise information on the activities of the hostiles south of the border. Willcox had his spy or spies in Mexico, and so did Mackenzie. Later on, other means of extracting information were attempted.

Hatch knew the difficulty of maintaining troops along the border in southern New Mexico because of lack of water. Yet appreciating the necessity for so doing if the hostiles making raids were to be headed off, he had urged early in 1881 that a deal be made with the Mexicans for a picket post at Palomas, where there was water, about five miles south of the line below present-day Columbus.[1] Nothing came of this suggestion. A month later he reported his commands doing the best they could to protect the frontier, while Terrazas was active with about one hundred men in the Janos–Carrizal area where Victorio had been accustomed to operate.[2] But, as we have seen, Nana breezed right through such screens and completed a destructive raid despite them. Others no doubt would try.

Hatch's sources of information from Mexico apparently

[1] LS95DNM1881 Hatch to AAG, Fort Leavenworth, March 11, 1881.
[2] LS153DNM1881 Hatch to AAG, Fort Leavenworth, April 19, 1881.

had been sketchy, but Mackenzie was not satisfied with that. When Mackenzie took over, he set about at once to improve matters. He secured accurate information from George B. Zimpleman, "a reliable man and largely interested in silver mines and stock raising," who lived near Corralitos, above Casas Grandes, Chihuahua.[3] But his principal source of information was Van Ness Cummings Smith, known to Southwesterners everywhere as Van C. Smith, an intelligent and trustworthy man of wide experience.[4] Smith had been sent into Mexico by Colonel Luther Prentice Bradley, when Bradley had been temporarily in command of the district of southern New Mexico. Mackenzie realized at once Smith's value as a scout. Mackenzie believed Smith's reports were "entirely truthful" and said he would send Smith once more into Mexico "to watch the Indians and forward information."[5] He ordered Forsyth to direct Smith south "with instructions to ascertain present location of the hostile Indians, and secure all possible information relative to their movements. Should he discover any movement of the Indians from Mexico, direct him to . . .

[3] LS169DNM1882 Dorst to Noyes, Fort Craig, March 19, 1882; LS184DNM1882 Mackenzie to Richard Hudson, Hot Springs, March 25, 1882; LS192DNM1882 Mackenzie to Pope, Fort Leavenworth, March 28, 1882; LS789DA1882 Mackenzie to Willcox, March 26, 1882.

[4] Born at Ludlow, Windsor County, Vermont, July 12, 1837, Smith died at Prescott on August 29, 1914. He was the founder of Roswell, N.M., naming it for his father, Roswell Smith. He never married. He was best known for his pioneering in Arizona. He arrived in the Prescott area late in the summer of 1863 (Prescott was founded in 1864), was a rancher and held various official positions. He was at Tombstone shortly after it was founded, served as an army Chief of Scouts at various times, and mined in Old Mexico. He was the first sheriff in pioneer Arizona, served as deputy under Sheriff John Behan at Tombstone, and was regarded as a worthy pioneer in every respect. Hayden Collections, Arizona Pioneers' Historical Society.

[5] LS494DNM1881 confidential Mackenzie to AAG, Fort Leavenworth, December 3, 1881.

69

telegraph full information. . . . Scout Smith will be allowed as heretofore $100.00 a month . . . in addition to that amount 50 cents per day for service of his horse."[6]

Based on a report from Smith in January, Mackenzie sent detailed instructions to Forsyth, at Fort Cummings, on how he was to operate in the case of a raid. Mackenzie's instructions reveal something of the problems commanders then faced dealing with hostiles such as the Apaches.

In case these Indians come anywhere where you can get a chance at them spare no trouble to hurt them. If they are driven out by the Mexicans the opportunity will be good as they will be much worn. If any opportunity affords to co-operate with the Mexicans, do so fully. For example, if they should follow Indians to the line and be out of supplies, issue them rations. Also, if you can accomplish results by disregarding Department lines, do not hesitate to go into Arizona after them. . . . If you are hotly in pursuit and find that you must have mounted Indians to get along fast, do not hesitate to mount the necessary Yuma or Mojave trailers (five or six) on Cavalry horses and send the men dismounted to the nearest post or Railroad station. . . .

The gist is this: Do not try to do anything unless a fair opportunity offers and just as long as you can nurse your men and horses. If you have *the chance*, do not spare men or horseflesh to accomplish a result.

Of course I do not wish you in Arizona except in case of necessity, but should you get after them follow as fast as you can and to the San Carlos Reserve where they will probably go, in which case your presence there would aid materially in effecting their arrest.

You had best . . . get someone (if you have a really good Mexican packer he would be a good man) down on the Mexican

[6] LS497DNM1881 confidential Loud to Forsyth, Fort Cummings, December 4, 1881.

Horseshoe Canyon, New Mexico (center). Forsyth's fight with Loco took place against the high ridge in the left half of the picture, the Indians finally escaping over the top of the ridge and down the other side into Doubtful Canyon and the San Simon Valley. Forsyth called the site "the roughest I ever saw."

From positions high on the side of Horseshoe Canyon, the Apaches looked out over the entry to the canyon far below. Forsyth's cavalrymen swept up the terrain seen here, but could not fight their way up the cliffs to the Indians' position. The troops finally withdrew.

Doubtful Canyon, down which Loco led his people toward
Mexico, leads west to the San Simon Valley.

Stein's Peak Range, with Doubtful Canyon directly ahead. Loco's people came out of the mountains and escaped to the south. This picture is from San Simon Valley, looking northeast.

Loco's people were dancing around their camp at the springs (point 1) when they were fired upon by Darr's scouts placed along the ridge (point 2). The Indians fled south to the rocky hillock (point 3), where they made a successful stand, although the fight lasted most of the day.

This picture was taken from the positions on "Darr's Ridge" from which Lieutenant Darr's scouts fired on Loco's people on the rocky hill in the center. Apache gun positions were found on the hill, on the side facing the ridge. Cartridge cases were found both on the ridge, near where the picture was taken, and on the hill where Loco's people were beseiged.

Tupper's command came down out of the San Luis Mountains, probably through the canyon in the center of the picture, on the trail of Loco and his fleeing people. Tupper's troops fought the Indians across the broad valley to the southwest.

The García-Loco fight took place about where the cloud shadow crosses Aliso Creek in the center of the picture. In this action more than three-score Apaches were killed, most of them women and children, along with a number of Mexican soldiers. The area is north of the Sierra Madre.

line in their little towns to give you information if possible of when and where the Indians are likely to cross. . . .

There are not to exceed 140 Apache men now in the state of Sonora and you are likely to find 75 together should they cross. P.S. In my judgment, if they cross the New Mexican line, they will be most apt to strike through the country near Richmond [present-day Virden, N.M.] and follow the general course of the Gila through the mountains. . . . However . . . no one can foretell the movements of a band of Indians. . . . Get everything in order and watch through spies.[7]

The perceptive Mackenzie was exactly correct in his prediction of the route likely to be followed by the hostiles, as events demonstrated. But it was another thing to stop them.

Willcox, meanwhile, remained most hopeful of Mexican assistance. "If we can get the Mexicans to attack them, we may be able with the help of Mackenzie's troops to exterminate the tribe," he messaged a field commander.[8] No one knew for sure where the Chiricahuas were. A "reliable man" who left Casas Grandes on December 8 told First Lieutenant Frederick A. Smith down along the border that the "Chiricahuas have left there and gone to the Mountains north, becoming suspicious of the action of Mexican authorities. Man said they had gone Chiricahua Mountains. [Thomas J.] Jeffords thinks Sierra Madre."[9] In March they were reported around Corralitos, Chihuahua, "in great numbers."[10] Later that month they were reported near Janos, a major trading

[7] LS25DNM1882 Mackenzie to Forsyth, Fort Cummings, January 12, 1882.

[8] No serial number. Smith AAAG to Major George B. Sanford, Fort Bowie, November 22, 1881.

[9] LS4705DA1881 Smith to AAG, Whipple Barracks, December 14, 1881.

[10] LS169DNM1882 Dorst to Major Henry Noyes, Fort Craig, March 19, 1882.

center in Chihuahua, not far from Casas Grandes.[11] They were said to be seeking a local peace with the Mexicans, which Mackenzie thought they might arrange, although not with officials of Chihuahua who were more bitter against them. He was not quite convinced, however, that the report reaching him was entirely accurate.[12]

Meanwhile, the rumors of returning bands of hostiles, or perhaps messengers from those in Mexico to their kinsmen on San Carlos, grew more circumstantial.

On New Year's Day, the field officers in the south were warned about "rumors of hostile Indians attempting to return to Arizona" and urged to use "utmost watchfulness" and be ready to move out at a moment's notice.[13] On January 12, the commanding officer at Bowie was again urged to "keep a sharp lookout" and if possible to use veteran scout Al Sieber.[14] In a subsequent directive, the commander at Bowie was ordered to "hold the troops under your command at all times in readiness to strike the Chiricahuas if they come within striking distance either in Arizona or New Mexico. A hearty cooperation with the Mexican troops . . . is strictly enjoined. . . . If any post or field comdr has a chance he will not wait for orders or spare men or horseflesh." It said that Major David Perry, 6th Cavalry, a veteran Indian fighter with experience in the Northwest as well as in the Southwest, was assigned to command field operations in southeastern Arizona.[15] Some elusive information concerning the escaped Bonito was channeled by a secret informant through the commanding officer

[11] LS191DNM1882 Mackenzie to Fuero, Chihuahua, March 28, 1882.

[12] LS192DNM1882 Mackenzie to Pope, Fort Leavenworth, March 28, 1882.

[13] LS2DA1881 Benjamin to C.O., Fort Huachuca, Fort Bowie, January 1, 1882.

[14] LS81DA1882 Benjamin to C.O., Fort Bowie, January 12, 1882.

[15] LS117DA1882 Benjamin to C.O., Fort Bowie, January 20, 1882.

at Camp Thomas and relayed to Willcox, but apparently nothing came of it.[16]

Early in February hostiles were reported to have killed a white man in the Dragoons, northeast of Tombstone and across the Sulphur Springs Valley from the mighty Chiricahua uplift. Tombstone papers thought these might be San Carlos Indians en route south to join the errant Chiricahuas in Mexico. However, Second Lieutenant John Y. F. Blake, with a 6th Cavalry patrol and ten scouts under Sieber, scoured the range from end to end and found no hostiles at all.[17] Other false reports alleged atrocities in Aravaipa Canyon, east of Fort Grant.[18] Everyone was on edge. Captain Tullius C. Tupper of the 6th Cavalry reported from San Bernardino, in the extreme southeastern corner of Arizona, that he had found a trail of about "forty Indians crossing Guadalupe Cañon . . . coming from direction of Stein's Peak Range." Subsequent investigation showed this trail was made by Second Lieutenant Charles S. Hall of the 13th Infantry and a company of Indian scouts from New Mexico.[19]

Yet not all the rumors were unfounded, or figments of someone's over-lively imagination. The hostiles were busy. They had not forgotten their San Carlos friends.

Major Perry was warned in late February that "it is important to keep the border scouted." The message, from Willcox's headquarters, added more ominously, "Indian In-

16 LS279DA1882 Benjamin to C.O., Camp Thomas, February 8, 1882.

17 LS603DA1882 Willcox to AAG, Military Division of the Pacific, February 9, 1882; LS657DA1882 Benjamin to Perry, Fort Bowie, February 10, 1882; LS669DA1882 Willcox to Governor Tritle, Tucson, February 11, 1882; LS367DA1882 Willcox to AG, Washington, February 16, 1882.

18 LS384DA1882 Willcox to AG, Washington, February 17, 1882.

19 LS322DA1882 Willcox to Mackenzie, Santa Fe, February 13, 1882; LS352DA1882 Mackenzie to Willcox, Whipple Barracks, February 14, 1882.

spector Howard reports that the Warm Spring Indians at San Carlos admit visit of six hostile Chiricahuas as reported." The Warm Springs Apaches were under the leadership of Loco, a wise and venerable former lieutenant of Victorio, a man who inclined toward peace, but who stoutly led his people through all their coming vicissitudes as befitted an able and conscientious leader. The Chiricahuas, Howard reported, were "emissaries," not simple visitors, and they came bearing threats.[20] According to one well-informed historian, these implacable hostiles bluntly informed Loco that Juh and Nachez would swing north on a raid within forty days, or early in April, and would force Loco and his people out of San Carlos and lead them southward to the Sierra Madre.[21] If this report is true, they kept their word.

More temporary military camps were established in southern Arizona,[22] but they were to prove as ineffectual as the others. The *Tombstone Epitaph* reported optimistically that the Mexicans were to start out major forces against the Sierra Madre Apaches, but the officers did not place too much reliance upon such tales,[23] although apparently these were not entirely baseless.

Late in March, Zimpleman wired Mackenzie from Corralitos that "Ju, Apache Chief, here. Think he will go for San Carlos. Has stolen 93 head of horses and mules from me. He

[20] LS378DA1882 Benjamin to Perry, February 19, 1882; LS384DA1882 Willcox to AG, Washington, February 17, 1882, which includes telegram, Howard to Willcox, reporting threats; LS386DA1882 Willcox to Mackenzie, Santa Fe, February 20, 1882.

[21] Lockwood, *The Apache Indians*, 246–47.

[22] LS400DA1882 Benjamin to Perry, Fort Bowie, February 21, 1882; LS747DA1882 Benjamin to Tiffany, San Carlos, March 22, 1882; LS751DA1882 Benjamin to Perry, Camp Thomas, March 22, 1882.

[23] LS761DA1882 Willcox to Mackenzie, Santa Fe, March 24, 1882.

has eight captured American children."[24] Zimpleman was correct in his surmise, for Juh went north by way of the Stein's Peak Range and the Gila, entering the immense San Carlos reserve where he visited with the outlaw Na-ti-o-tish on Eagle Creek.[25] Then with his fellow hostiles, Juh slipped down the river toward San Carlos intent upon precipitating yet another major uprising.

Their route had already been discovered by Sieber and a scouting party, as he later reported to Willcox. He said that the breakout of the Warm Springs Indians, soon to take place, "was premeditated ever since the Chiricahua Indians left the Reservation last fall," when the Warm Springs, he believed, intended to go, too, but were prevented by the proximity of numerous troops.

"The Chiricahuas have been holding communication with them, during the last winter to my certain knowledge and the way they have held their communication was by coming up on the eastern side of the Stein's Peak Range of Mountains from Old Mexico, this being the only available route by which they could communicate, without danger to themselves from troops scouting along the line." Sieber reported he had been scouting along the Arizona–New Mexico border with Sonora and Chihuahua in late March and early April when "I, on the north end of the Las Animas Mts. discovered fresh Indian signs of the Chiricahuas making their way toward the San Carlos Agency . . . , although before I could send this information to the troops in time to be of any benefit, I heard of their having left the Reservation."[26]

[24] LS789DA1882 Willcox to AAG, Military Division of the Pacific, March 26, 1882.
[25] LS1155DA1882 MacGowan to C.O., Fort Apache, included in Willcox to AAG, Military Division of the Pacific, April 27, 1882.
[26] LS2924DA1882 Sieber to Willcox, Whipple Barracks, June 8, 1882.

75

VII LET OUR PEOPLE GO!

Ripples of unrest preceded or accompanied the movement of Juh's hostiles toward San Carlos, as Indians as far distant as Fort Apache, a full week before the blowup, reported that an outbreak had occurred at San Carlos.[1] Those rumors were false, but they forecast the event to come.

On Wednesday, April 19, Major Samuel N. Benjamin, assistant adjutant general, messaged appropriate post commanders, relaying advice from the subagency, nineteen or twenty miles east of San Carlos, that: "Sheever's band at Sub Agency four men and about thirty women and children skipped last night. This morning Chief of Police Sterling went to see if Warm Springs Indians near Agency were all right. Sterling was killed and all of Loco's band left after killing him. Chiricahuas threaten to kill every one at Sub Agency, and here today or tonight. Suggest Troops be sent at once."[2] But it was too late.

Jason Betzinez, an Apache boy just under warrior age at the time of this exodus, said that it was the "warriors," that

---

[1] LS932DA1882 Benjamin to Tiffany, San Carlos, April 11, 1882; LS933DA1882 Benjamin to Tiffany, San Carlos, April 11, 1882.

[2] LS966DA1882 Benjamin to C.O., Fort Apache, April 19, 1882.

is, the Apaches from Mexico, who had killed Sterling and Sagotal, an Indian policeman with him, and not Loco's band.[3] This very likely was the case. Juh had led his fighting men, who included Chihuahua, Nachez, Chatto, and perhaps Geronimo, the pick of the Chiricahua hostiles, racing past the subagency and on toward San Carlos, where, it was rumored, they intended to incite a general massacre of the whites. But the encounter with Sterling, who had been alerted by the subagency telegraph operator, caused them to change their minds, and they now boiled back to Loco's camp. Here, some said at rifle point, they forced Loco to lead his people out on the long trail toward Mexico.

The precise number of Apaches who fled the reservation in this great action is not certainly known. The number generally given is 700, perhaps including the Mexico hostiles who may have numbered anything from 8 to 40. George H. Stevens, veteran Arizona pioneer, married to an Apache and fluent in that tongue, estimated there were 90 warriors in the party, which would have made the total group 400 or 500 people.[4] Willcox said that various estimates put the number of hostiles at 150 to 200, meaning warriors alone, which would bring the total to nearly 700.[5] Lieutenant Haskell, who as aide to Willcox had accumulated great experience in dealing with those Indians now hostile, favored the lower estimate and wondered "is there no one with that force who will hit the hostiles?"[6] Sherman, rumbling in his customary belligerent man-

3 Jason Betzinez to author, November 10, 1959.

4 LS1085DA1882 Haskell to Perry, Willcox, April 21, 1882.

5 LS1090DA1882 Willcox to AAG, Military Division of the Pacific, April 21, 1882; LS1121DA1882 Willcox to Mexican Consul, Tucson, April 24, 1882.

6 LS1085DA1882 Haskell to C.O. Scouting Operations, Willcox, April 21, 1882.

ner, ordered that "all troops should go for them and attack them regardless of relative forces."[7]

But it was the enemy who held the initiative.

The problem for Juh and Loco was to find a way over hundreds of miles of troop-infested desert, where even a circling hawk could be seen for a score of miles, into the Mexico sanctuary with a horde of women, children, and old people, as well as livestock and warriors. It would have appeared an impossible task to any but Apaches, although so sudden and so overwhelming was the break that it caught the Southwest almost unprepared.

The multitude fled eastward along the course of the Gila. The noncombatants traveled mostly north of the river, in the broken country, while the warriors under Juh and the others ranged widely, leaving the path of their flight littered with more than fifty dead whites, looted and burned freight wagons, plundered ranches, and slain herdsmen. Sheep were stolen to feed the people, and most of the slayings were done to acquire guns, ammunition, or other desperately needed resources. Numerous bodies of troops pursued them, but none pushed on to the point of contact with so large a body of enemy.[8]

"None of our Warm Springs Apaches had weapons," recalled Betzinez. "We were helpless in the hands of the Netdahe [Southern Apaches]. . . . We were filled with gloom and despair."[9] He described the movement eastward through the mountains north of the river. The flight continued all the first day and first night, when some of the warriors swung wide to collect sheep for food at the Stevens' ranch, where

[7] *Ibid.*

[8] See Thrapp, *Conquest of Apacheria*, 236–40, for detailed account.

[9] Jason Betzinez, *I Fought With Geronimo*, 56–57.

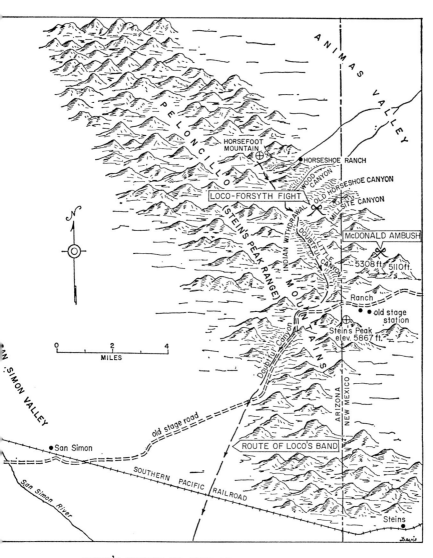

LOCO'S ROUTE TO THE SAN SIMON VALLEY

they killed seven men, one woman, and two children and stole an estimated $5,000 worth of the animals.[10] The band camped two days, gorging on mutton while the countryside was scoured by troops looking for them. "The Chiricahuas and Warm Spring Indians are murdering citizens in the Upper Gila," Willcox wired San Francisco, charging that Geronimo was with the enemy.[11]

"It was realized that the band would have to make better time somehow if they wanted to escape into Mexico," wrote Betzinez. "Therefore several men were sent north along the San Francisco River to raid a ranch for some horses and mules which the women and children could ride."[12] Others were dispatched on similar missions in other directions.

Once mounted, the movement gained momentum. After a long night march the party found water in the Stein's Peak Range. Watered, it moved "halfway up the mountain," on what apparently was the south side of Old Horseshoe Canyon, while a dozen warriors were sent southeast "on a scouting expedition." It was they who precipitated the first action between the Loco band and the troops.

Aware that the Indians likely would sweep south through the Stein's Peak Range, Forsyth, whose base camp was at Separ, a railroad siding twenty miles east of Lordsburg, planned to take his four companies of cavalry and one of infantry westerly for Stein's Pass, where the Southern Pacific loops around the south end of the range. "All my information tends to show Indians went up through range and will go down the same way," he wired Willcox, although Mac-

[10] LS1058DA1882 Scully to AAG, Whipple Barracks, April 20, 1882.
[11] LS1090DA1882 Willcox to AAG, Military Division of the Pacific, April 21, 1882.
[12] Betzinez, *I Fought With Geronimo*, 60.

kenzie was his own department commander.[13] He moved his command by railroad, watered it with great difficulty at Stein's, a siding at the pass, and messaged Willcox again early on Saturday that "I leave here in an hour on a trail of ten Indians reported crossing railroad six miles east of here last night. Believe them to be advance guard of outbreaking Indians, who are on the way to Mexico. Shall take the back trail unless I find the main body have crossed the railroad."[14] The trail, however, had been left by the party of twelve warriors, Betzinez reported, who had killed a track walker on the railway, scouted the line for troops, and now were en route back to the main band in Horseshoe Canyon. Forsyth ordered Lieutenant McDonald with six mounted scouts and two enlisted men to follow the trail north through the uplift, while he took his larger command across the extensive flats between the range and Lordsburg, northeast toward Richmond, now Virden, on the Gila.[15]

When approximately in the mouth of East Doubtful Canyon, McDonald's party was ambushed and four scouts slain. The enemy did not press their advantage, however, and when Forsyth with his several companies swept up to the rescue, they withdrew, behind a choking grass fire they had set, to rejoin their comrades high on the south side of Horseshoe Canyon. Forsyth attacked the party there, in the first major engagement between Loco and the troops during this flight.

Horseshoe Canyon is a wide-mouthed gorge, debouching toward the northeast. Its highest and steepest side is on the south, topped by a 6,500-foot unnamed mountain which sep-

[13] LS1799DA1882 Forsyth to Willcox, Whipple Barracks, April 21, 1882.

[14] LS1101DA1882 Forsyth to Willcox, Whipple Barracks, April 22, 1882.

[15] For details of McDonald's scout, the ambush, and Forsyth's rescue and the battle in Horseshoe Canyon, see Thrapp, *Conquest of Apacheria*, 240–45.

arates it from Little Doubtful Canyon. The latter leads southerly and opens into Doubtful Canyon proper about at Stein's Peak. Horseshoe is a bony, barren defile. Attacking an enemy situated on its high southern side would present a monumental task indeed.

The colonel found them "strongly entrenched on the left side of Horse Shoe Cañon, and also in the middle of it." Major Wirt Davis rounded up a number of the hostiles' ponies, while other elements pushed the assault. "In about an hour we compelled them to abandon their position and fall back," wrote Forsyth. "They then took up a second strong position, which we again flanked them out of, and gradually drove them back into the cañon and up among the high peaks of the range, some of them firing at us from points eight, twelve, and even sixteen hundred feet above us. I never saw a more rugged place."

He added that "the air was suffocatingly hot in the cañon, and we were weary and very thirsty. On one side of the cañon, near its head, was a small spring trickling into a pool in the rocks, and no sooner was it discerned than it was surrounded by men with canteens, while others drank from the brim of their campaign hats, and again others threw themselves flat on their faces and lapped up the water. . . . Like a flash came the crack of five or six rifles. . . . The way that thirsty crowd broke for cover was astonishing."[16]

[16] Forsyth tells the story of this campaign, including the battle of Horseshoe Canyon and later events in his *Thrilling Days in Army Life*, 79–121. The spring is on the west side of the canyon, which is more accurately an indentation on the side of the mountain than a "canyon" as is generally understood. Near this spring I found two cartridge cases of the period, indicating that the soldiers had returned the enemy's fire, at least perfunctorily. Forsyth was accurate in his estimate of the elevation of the Indian positions above the attackers. It would have been virtually impossible for the soldiers to have

With the Indians out of reach, Forsyth withdrew his battered forces to the Gila. His casualties included three soldiers besides the four scouts slain, an officer and four privates wounded. Though he must have been aware that the Indians, bound for Mexico, would utilize watered Doubtful Canyon, Forsyth failed to dispatch part of his heavy force to picket that defile, and so permitted the enemy to escape. He thought he had killed two of them and maintained that he had "won" the engagement, but Southwesterners wrathfully denied this and accused Forsyth of faint heart in not pressing his attack when he had the enemy at bay.[17]

With the white disengagement, the Indians withdrew over the high mountain and slipped into Little Doubtful Canyon, down it to the main arroyo, and across the hump, slipping unmolested down West Doubtful for the broad San Simon Valley, which they crossed that night, making for the Chiricahua uplift, the ancestral home of the Apache band of that name. This was what Willcox and Perry, commanding in southeastern Arizona, expected them to do. Perry was warned not to permit it, but he was helpless to divert the Indians, although he did the next best thing.

"Have you taken precaution to learn if hostiles go through between Stein's Peak Range and Bowie?" demanded Haskell, speaking for Willcox, in a message to Perry, who was con-

routed the enemy under their plan of attack, although with competent guides it might have been feasible for men to get above and behind the enemy by way of Doubtful Canyon. This was not attempted. Perhaps Forsyth was not aware that there was good water in Doubtful Canyon.

[17] See "Military and Indians: Al Seiber Tells What He Knows About the Late War," in the *Prescott Weekly Courier*, May 27, 1882, for a seasoned opinion on the Forsyth fight, as well as primary details in the next major actions to come in this Loco campaign. Where it can be checked against other sources, the Sieber version has proved reliable.

cerned with nothing else. Haskell urged a close patrol of the railroad line, including a detachment moving on handcars, to check against the Apaches' crossing the tracks heading south. Willcox "thinks it would be best to have a Cavalry and Scout Co. on the east side of the Chiricahuas below Bowie. . . . I need not repeat the General's anxiety that your troops shall make a hit. While concentrating for the blow north of the railroad, any Indian marauders to the south of it must be annihilated and not allowed to reach the Mexican line."[18]

Forsyth too messaged Perry that the Indians had escaped toward the Chiricahua range and Old Mexico, and that he was on the trail after fighting them in the Stein's Peak Range. He had picked up Captain Charles G. Gordon and his 6th Cavalry troop. Captain Adna Romanza Chaffee prepared to leave Fort Bowie to intercept their trail on the other side of Apache Pass. First Lieutenant Frank West, also of the 6th Cavalry, would join him with another troop.[19] But better centered on the action were two veteran 6th Cavalry troops, those commanded by Captain Tupper and Captain William C. Rafferty, both Indian fighters of long experience, along with Companies M and D of Indian Scouts, under Lieutenant Darr and Second Lieutenant Stephen C. Mills, both of the 12th Infantry. By reason of rank Captain Tupper was in over-all command.[20] With the outfit was Sieber, the best of all Arizona chiefs of scouts of the period, and Pat Keogh, along with the necessary pack trains operated by experienced and durable civilian packers. Among these it is possible that Tom

18 LS1107DA1882 Haskell to Perry, Willcox, April 23, 1882.

19 LS1128DA1882 Willcox to AAG, Military Division of the Pacific, quoting field dispatches from Forsyth, Chaffee, and Perry, April 25, 1882.

20 LS1138DA1882 Willcox to AAG, Military Division of the Pacific, April 26, 1882.

Horn, later a controversial figure in the West, was numbered.[21]

Tupper messaged at 9 A.M. on April 25 that he "arrived at Galeyville [on the east slope of the Chiricahuas] about 3 A.M. Rafferty joined and trail of seventy or eighty animals [was discovered] soon after sunrise, possibly thirty or forty Indians. They crossed [San Simon] Valley, trail running southeast last night. Shall remain here until evening. Then make as long a night march as possible. The only show I can see, but think it impossible we can overtake them before they get into Mexico unless they loiter in camp."[22]

The main body of Indians had trekked down the broad valley, but a raiding force swept up toward Galeyville, attacking its outskirts and slaying a deputy sheriff, then curved back to join the larger body. This was the trail Tupper had seen. Meanwhile, there were reports of enemies, Indians, hostiles, and suspicious people everywhere in southeastern Arizona and southwestern New Mexico. Some were excitedly rumored to be on the west slope of the Chiricahuas, where none were in actuality; others were said to be elsewhere. A telegraph operator at Tombstone, with an urgent dispatch for Camp Rucker, at the southern end of the Chiricahuas, could get no messenger with the courage to deliver it.[23] One small party of hostiles killed two men near Ayres Camp, a place

[21] Al Sieber wrote that Horn went to work in the government pack trains in 1882, no doubt during this campaign. See statement in Tom Horn, *A Vindication: Life of Tom Horn By Himself*, 311. In this book, which probably was heavily edited or rewritten from a draft Horn may have worked up while in prison, he describes the ensuing actions in a way which gives little doubt of personal knowledge of them on his part, although he was not yet a scout as he claims to have been. See 74–93.

[22] LS1138DA1882 *op. cit.*

[23] *Ibid.*

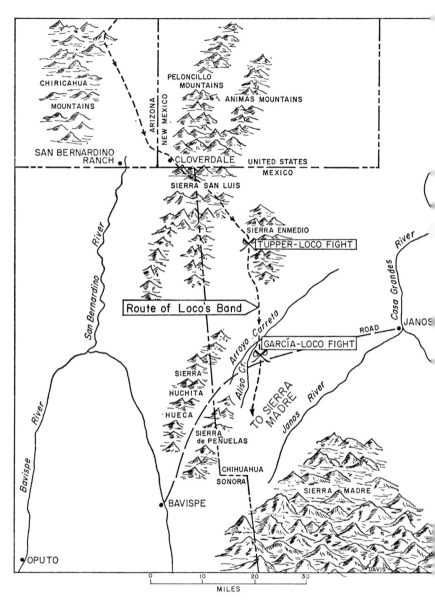

LOCO'S ROUTE FROM THE CHIRICAHUA MOUNTAINS TO
ALISO CREEK

apparently on Pinery Creek in the Chiricahuas, but hurried south before they could be intercepted.[24] They were not heard from again, and no doubt entered Mexico without incident. With dusk Tupper and his augmented command slipped down onto the floor of the valley, in pursuit of the fleeing main party of Indians.[25] The following morning, Perry reported to Willcox, Forsyth reached Galeyville and left almost immediately with his large party, "moving towards Mexico."[26] Thus there were three parties now strung out on the long trail: the hostiles, several hundred strong; Tupper's command of 107 men, less than one-quarter the size of the enemy band; and Forsyth's command of about 450 men, perhaps, at least double the greatest number of Indian warriors that had been estimated. Tupper's command followed the plain trail southeasterly, toward Cloverdale, in extreme southwestern New Mexico, beyond the stony Peloncillo Mountains which bound the San Simon Valley to the east. Sieber reported that they marched "at a trot and gallop for about thirty miles. At this point the hostiles scattered so the trail disappeared." They struck the Peloncillos at 3 A.M., waited until daylight, crossed the range at five thousand feet and by 6 P.M. were encamped a few miles north of Cloverdale, starting out once more at 4:30 A.M. on April 27. They crossed into Old Mexico, pushing south along the western face of the Sierra de San Luis,

[24] LS1155DA1882 Willcox to AAG, Military Division of the Pacific, April 27, 1882.

[25] In addition to Sieber's, Forsyth's, and Horn's accounts, Rafferty's diary of this campaign was printed in the *Arizona Star*, May 17, 1882, and Darr's long and useful interview was printed on May 26, 1882. These are the principal sources for the story here told, unless otherwise cited. For a more extended version of the pursuit and fight, see Thrapp, *Al Sieber, Chief of Scouts*, 225–43.

[26] LS1155DA1882 Willcox to AAG, Military Division of the Pacific, April 27, 1882.

generally south of the Peloncillos. The Apaches had broken trail through clinging manzanita and chaparral, which had cruelly delayed them, and the troopers gained rapidly. The way then led over the seven thousand-foot summit on no trail at all. "This proved a terrible hard pull for the boys," Rafferty conceded, in his diary. They came down a sweeping canyon on the eastern slope, with the enemy trail freshening every mile. By 6 P.M. they had traveled thirty-five difficult miles, rested two and one-half hours, then set out again, leaving their pack train in camp. The enemy must now be close. "The trail at this point was very fresh," wrote Rafferty.

The canyon they probably descended opens onto a level valley, perhaps five or six miles wide, between the San Luis and the next mountain system to the east, the Sierra Enmedio, which the whites called "Middle Mountain," as the name properly translates. About in the center of this range, and at its western base, lay a good spring with abundant water, a spring that still exists. The Apaches knew it well, as had countless generations of Indians before them. Ruins lately excavated in its vicinity show that a more sedentary tribe had dwelled in the vicinity of the water for ages past, although there were no such people living there in 1882. About 200 yards to the north, or a little farther, lay two rocky hillocks, west of the main range, and about 150 yards to the south of the spring lay another single hill, also rocky and "very rough" as contemporary accounts have it. Behind the spring, along the base of the mountains, was a ridge, running north and south, perhaps 40 or 50 feet in height and 200 or 300 yards distant from the spring. From it one could command the rocky protuberances to the north and south of the water.

Sieber led the advance with ten scouts from the resting place out onto the flat valley, now shrouded with darkness.

Darr said his instructions were "to locate the Indian camp if possible." A mile and a half behind them came the balance of the Indian scouts, and three miles to the rear was the main column of cavalry, "held back to avoid routing the hostiles by the clatter of hoofs, or other noise made by horses."

Five miles from the camp the Apache fires were sighted by the advance party, and Darr and Mills crawled up from their position with the main body of scouts. Pat Keogh was told to await Captain Tupper, advising him to hold up, pending further word from the advance. Darr sent Sieber and four Indians to reconnoiter ahead. They returned within an hour, reported that there seemed to be about 115 warriors, and that the enemy camp was "making medicine." This was good news, and word was sent to Tupper, who then came up.

The captain sent the two scout companies, totaling 47 men, under Sieber's guidance, to man the ridge behind the spring. He and Captain Rafferty would bring the troopers on across the plains to a position confronting the hostiles and eight hundred to one thousand yards distant.

Thus the enemy would be cut off from the mountains behind and the plains in front, and, it was hoped, could be finally trapped. The scouts got into position just before dawn, but their action was hastened when they were discovered by four Apaches, three women and a man. The scouts opened fire, killing all of them. Heavy fire was immediately concentrated on the enemy camp, which Darr estimated to be four hundred yards before them.

"This fusillade threw the hostile camp into confusion," Darr reported. Most of the Indians bounded for the rocky prominence to the south, first taking care to extinguish their fires. Lieutenant Bo Blake drove off much of the enemy's herd, under heavy fire, and the troopers formed a skirmish line and pressed toward the opponents' positions. Darr described the action:

> Both sides now kept up a continuous fire until a quarter of three o'clock p.m. At that hour, having been twenty-one hours without rations or water, and having but three rounds of ammunition to each man . . . it became absolutely necessary to withdraw, which they did in good order, to the place of their camp of the previous night, nine miles distant. . . .
>
> In about an hour after getting into camp Forsyth's command of eight companies of Cavalry and three companies of Indian scouts . . . arrived very unexpectedly, being well supplied with ammunition.

Forsyth, all eagerness, wanted to attack the Indians that night, but Tupper said his command was done in, and the senior officer did not wish to move into a hornet's nest without someone to show the way. By next morning, when the united command reapproached the scene of the fight, the Indians had gone. Sieber and others estimated that seventeen warriors had been killed in the Tupper fight and, although the scout was not aware of it, Loco himself had been wounded.[27]

[27] Betzinez, *I Fought With Geronimo*, 69. Betzinez, who was in this fight, although not yet a warrior, gives a graphic description of it from the Indian side, 68–70. I have surveyed the site from the air and twice searched it on the ground, finding relics of the action. Cartridge cases, flattened by roaming livestock, found at the head of the spring show that the Indians fired heavily back at their assailants as soon as the attack began. They then apparently dashed for the south hill. Midway between the spring and the hill a companion, John A. Shapard, found six cartridge cases from a .44-caliber revolver, indicating that a hostile had rapidly reloaded his weapon at that point. On Darr's ridge, behind the scene, were found piles of empty cartridge cases, left by the scouts who shot up their ammunition at the hostiles on Loco's hill. The hill itself seems to have been gone over in the past, but we found, with the help of James Walker's metal detector, lead slugs and cartridge cases, as well as several hasty fortifications constructed of broken rock, erected by the Apaches during the action.

VIII GARCÍA'S AMBUSH

Loco must have gathered his people and taken them out of the Enmedio Mountain position about dusk, because by dawn they were twenty-nine miles south, almost across the Janos Plains (which here are level as a tabletop) and approaching the Sierra Madre, dimly visible on the southern horizon beyond the nearer bluffs. It was here that they were struck once more, for the third major time on their epic exodus, and had their most disastrous battle. It was not, however, with American forces, but with Mexican.

Betzinez said that the march was a difficult one, because the people were tired and worn out and had to rest at least once during the night. Some, who were mounted, including Ka-ya-ten-nae, Chatto, and Nachez, pushed on ahead and, when they saw some Mexican soldiers, were afraid to come back and tell the horde and went on into the foothills. Others, who were ahead of the movement as security, stopped "to have a smoke," perhaps because they also had seen Mexicans in the advance. The people on foot passed them and went on, into the jaws of the trap.

"When we had gone a few hundred yards we were suddenly attacked by Mexican soldiers who came at us out of the ravine where they had been concealed," remembered Betzinez. "Almost immediately Mexicans were right among us all, shooting down women and children right and left. Here and there a few Indian warriors were running in all directions. It was a dreadful, pitiful sight." Geronimo and Chihuahua, he said, rallied thirty-two warriors to protect the band. Those who escaped owed their lives to this action, for these warriors put up a determined resistance and, supplied with plenty of ammunition, caused the Mexicans most of the casualties they suffered.[1]

Sieber, who examined the field next day, wrote:

> as far as I was able to see there were eleven bucks and plenty of squaws and children killed, and fourteen squaws and eleven children captured. The Mexicans had twenty-three killed and about thirty wounded. More bucks may have been killed, but I failed to see them. As soon as [Colonel Lorenzo] Garcia opened fire all of Juh's bucks and the young bucks belonging to the Warm Spring band put spurs to their horses and made escape. The old bucks stood and fought for their families and there they died with them. Young bucks look out for themselves— old bucks fight for their families.[2]

García's fight was reported by Brigadier José Guillermo Carbo, commandant of the First Military Zone, which included Sonora, Baja California, Sinaloa, and Tepic, in a communication to the secretary of war and marine, in which he said that it occurred at 6 A.M. on April 29.

> In the Arroyo a las Alvios [Alivos, or Alisos], state of Chihuahua, the two columns under command of Colonel Lorenzo Garcia and Major Luis Cherono united and defeated completely a marauding band of Apaches that came from the United States

[1] Betzinez, *I Fought With Geronimo*, 70–75.
[2] "Military and Indians," *Prescott Weekly Courier*, May 27, 1882.

. . . and killed seventy-five and twenty-two wounded women were captured. . . . This cost us the death of 6th Battalion First Captain Antonio Rada and ten soldiers of that organization, Guard Lieutenant of Bavispe Serapio Lugo and four soldiers of Bavispe and Bacerac, Second Lieutenant of the scouting force Ygnacio Franco, and four soldiers of the Sonoran auxiliary forces, having been wounded Major Heron, of the same corps, and Lieutenant Jesus Galicia of Bacerac.

The enlisted men wounded were neither named nor their number given.[3]

Colonel Forsyth, with his command now numbering nearly six hundred men, including the Apache scouts, moved south across the Janos Plains that same day, camped, and the next morning ran across the Mexican force under García, learning details of the previous day's battle. Physicians with his command provided professional services for García's wounded, but Forsyth, illegally in Mexico, since no treaty provision then authorized such a penetration, was invited in no uncertain terms to leave.

On April 30, García messaged thirty-two-year-old Brigadier General Bernardo Reyes at Bavispe:

Today at 10 a.m. I was starting my march toward that city [Bavispe] when I was advised of the proximity of an American force command by a Cavalry Lieutenant and 100 Apache soldiers [scouts] under command of General George A. Forsyth. As was natural, this invasion of our territory much surprised me, and I sent [Forsyth] the following communication:

"Please tell me what object has caused this unjustified invasion of Mexican territory. And at the same time please leave

3 114814/11874 Secretario de Guerra y Marina, 1882, entitled: Convenios en tropas Americanas y Mexicanas, respecto a la persecucion de los Indios hostiles . . . y otros diversos asuntos sobre los mismos bárbaros. Archivos de la Secretaria de la Defensa Nacional, 185–86.

our country, or I will be obliged, despite the small size of my
column, to repel [the invasion] with force, making you responsible for the grave consequences for both nations that will
result."

As a result of this note, the said General answered me with
a communication, the original of which accompanies this, and
he and his force have already retired from our territory.

Forsyth's note, which is filed with the García communication, acknowledged receipt of the Mexican's protest, and explained:

My object in entering upon Mexican Territory was the punishment of a band of Indians who assassinated numbers of citizens of the United States in Arizonia [sic] and New Mexico, and
stole great numbers of their animals. I followed these Indians
day and night thro' three Mountain Ranges, attacking and fighting them twice during the last eight days and was in full pursuit
of them this morning, when I met your command and was informed by you, that, yesterday the forces under your command
attacked and destroyed this force of Indians which I was in
pursuit of. Under these circumstances I am only too well satisfied to cease the pursuit of this band of Indians, and shall with-
draw my forces at once, from Mexican soil.

I congratulate yourself, and the Troops under your command,
for your brilliant victory of yesterday.[4]

Forsyth later told an interviewer at Lordsburg, New Mexico, that he had learned from a wounded Apache he believed
was Loco's son that the band had lost six men killed in the
Tupper fight and thirteen at Horseshoe Canyon, but he apparently misunderstood, for the facts were close to the reverse.[5] He also stated the belief that only thirty or forty
warriors had escaped with Loco from the García fight, al-

[4] *Ibid.*, p. 244–46.

though this, too, was more optimistic than the facts warranted.

No official report of the Forsyth–García meeting ever was filed in this country. Mackenzie, realizing the diplomatic furor that might follow revelation of the action, returned Forsyth's report to him, saying "it was not unlikely I might find myself in trouble for my action. However, if the Mexicans did not make a direct complaint to the State Department, he should not take action, as the result justified the end; but the less said about it the better."[6]

Yet, as we have seen, García did make such a formal report, and the question remains why the Mexicans did not follow through with an official protest. The reason can only be, I think, that negotiations were then far advanced for a treaty permitting such crossings when in "hot pursuit," and these forestalled a protest over such an incident at that late date. Forsyth was lucky.

[5] See Thrapp, *Conquest of Apacheria*, for discussion of these figures. Report of Forsyth's interview in Secretario de Guerra y Marina file, *op. cit.*, 198.

[6] Forsyth, *Thrilling Days in Army Life*, 121.

IX RETURN OF CROOK

Washington had reason to be unhappy about the state of affairs in the Southwest. Beginning with Cibecue, the Apaches had joined in a series of clashes that included the Chiricahua *émeute* and now the Loco exodus. This almost cleared the Arizona reservations of hostilely-inclined bands and at the same time placed in the Sierra Madre sanctuary of Old Mexico a strong, belligerent force that could bode only ill for the frontier for a long time to come.

Willcox had proved himself largely ineffectual in dealing with these people. Mackenzie, for one reason or another, had done little better, although his record showed that he was a fine combat commander when he had an enemy where he could hit him. But it took one operation still to convince Sherman and his advisers that a stronger and more experienced hand was required to correct the rapidly worsening situation.

This last development culminated in what became known as the Battle of Big Dry Wash. It involved the recalcitrant Na-ti-o-tish and his forty hostiles whom we left lurking in the distant recesses of the two large reservations. Among them, perhaps, were some of the mutinous scouts of the Cibecue incident.

The problem of the errant scouts and other hostiles left over from Cibecue had been uppermost in the minds of army officers of Arizona ever since that lamentable occurrence. Early in 1882 one of them, known to the official records only as "Scout No. Eleven," was captured, after a furious struggle, and taken from San Carlos to the brig at Camp Thomas, where he was confined. He had been arrested by agency police on the night of February 3, according to S. D. Pangburn, acting agent. Tiffany had left San Carlos for good.[1]

Scout No. Eleven told Pangburn that the other hostiles "will not come in and surrender themselves as long as there is a possibility of their being punished. In his capture," Pangburn added, "he fought desperately for liberty, plainly showing that it was not their intention to be easily taken."

Willcox directed Lieutenant Cruse, still in command of the scout company, to prepare charges against Eleven, "according to the evidence you may be able to obtain from [interpreter] Hurrle, the soldiers and others."[2] Willcox was informed in April that Juh and Geronimo had sent emissaries to the renegades, inviting them to join the Loco *émeute*. "It is also rumored that they have sent to the Navajoes advising them to break out," Captain MacGowan reported. He was commandant at Fort Apache.[3] There seems no reason to doubt that some contact was established between Juh and his wild and hostile band and the recalcitrants evading capture on the

[1] LS603DA1882 Willcox to AAG, Military Division of the Pacific, February 9, 1882.

[2] LS603DA1882 Benjamin to Cruse, Fort Apache, February 9, 1882.

[3] LS1090DA1882 Willcox to AAG, Military Division of the Pacific, April 21, 1882.

Fort Apache–San Carlos reservations. But apparently it did not come to anything; for some reason they declined to join the vast exodus.

Late in May, Willcox messaged Washington that

> some seventeen of the revolted scouts are still at large and supposed to be harboring in the White Mountain fastnesses somewhere within the limits of the San Carlos Reservation, and where it is a delicate matter for the troops to scout. In addition to these scouts there is a small band that never came in after the Cibicu fight, and probably the Indians who recently broke guard and escaped from San Carlos Agency. Captain MacGowan estimates them at about forty bucks [in all].... Their presence is a standing menace . . . and a nucleus for renegades. . . . The scouts are well armed, and those who have joined them—Gar and others, are among the boldest as well as the worst of the band.[4]

He urged a liberal reward be offered for the capture, dead or alive, of those who remained out. No reward was approved, however, by the War Department, which also frowned on the use of troops on the reservation because the Indian Bureau did not want them there. So the problem of the hostiles simmered, while nothing was done to ease or solve it.

On July 6, Willcox protested that he still was "awaiting further instructions," warning that lack of action by the military made "the Cibicu renegades gain encouragement to take the aggressive.... They must be met decisively or the dangers will greatly increase."[5] He was entirely correct, as he learned the following day.

Late on July 6, 1882, Colonel William R. Shafter, 1st Infantry, now commanding scouting operations in succession

---

[4] LS1739DA1882 Willcox to AG, Washington, May 30, 1882.

[5] LS2009DA1882 Willcox to AAG, Military Division of the Pacific, July 6, 1882.

to Perry in southeastern Arizona, messaged Willcox: "It is reported that Chief of Scouts [Colvig] and three of his men were killed this A.M. near San Carlos, said to be by renegades from Apache. Am I at liberty to put troops on the reservation if I think it necessary?"[6] The incident occurred while most of the soldiers and officers were in the small Arizona towns celebrating the Fourth of July with appropriate activities, but as a result of it, they hurried back to their posts. Minor as the incident appeared to be, it precipitated a considerable military operation and a battle that was to be the last major skirmish between troops and non-Chiricahua Apaches in the Southwest.

Pangburn confirmed the incident, and Shafter reported he had eleven companies of troops available but "will not make a move until called on by Agent or ordered to do so. The thing to do," he added, however, "is to go after them now, before they get a start." He said in a subsequent message that the telegraph line from San Carlos to Globe had been cut, with yards of wire ripped down and thrown into an arroyo. In still another message, he reported that among those who had fired on Colvig, four had been recognized. They included Na-ti-o-tish, his two brothers, and Arishey, another well-known Cibecue hostile.[7]

The campaign and battle of Big Dry Wash have often been described and, therefore, need not be related in detail here.[8] Troops mustered from Apache, McDowell, Verde, and other posts converged upon the hostiles, who had laid an ambush at the point where a trail from the Tonto Basin climbs up

[6] LS2017DA1882 Shafter to AAAG, Whipple Barracks, July 6, 1882.

[7] LS2017DA1882 Willcox to Chaffee, Fort McDowell, July 7, 1882.

[8] See Cruse, *Apache Days and After*, 158–72; Britton Davis, *The Truth About Geronimo*, 9–28; Lockwood, *The Apache Indians*, 248–55; Thrapp, *Al Sieber, Chief of Scouts*, 244–57.

over the Mogollon Rim. The trap was discovered by Sieber, and the troops chose to use it for the battle which took place on July 17. Sixteen or more Indians, among them Na-ti-o-tish, were killed, and the rest dispersed.[9] The survivors filtered back to the reservations, gradually melded with the tame Apaches there, and were never afterward importantly heard from as renegades.

In a subsequent message to Washington, Willcox named the civilians killed or wounded by Indians during the Big Dry Wash campaign and in related incidents. In view of traditions of considerable numbers having fallen victim, it is worth reciting the facts here.

On July 9, in an attack on McMillenville, not far from Globe, Frank Ross was wounded. The next day a man named Gleason and a Mexican, whose name was not known, were killed along the Salt River. On July 12, Charles Sigsbee and Louis Houdon were killed in the Tonto Basin, and the next day John Meadows was killed and his three sons wounded along the East Fork of the Verde River. In an unrelated incident, a teamster named Jacob Farren was killed by Chiricahuas near San Carlos on July 19. On about July 22 a Mexican teamster, whose name was not known, was killed near Clifton.[10] Despite the rumors of "scoures" of people slain

<hr/>

[9] Dispatches concerned with this fight include LS2012DA1882 ADC to Shafter, Fort Grant, July 7, 1882; LS2025DA1882 ADC to Shafter, Fort Grant, July 9, 1882; LS2026DA1882 ADC to Chaffee, Fort McDowell, July 9, 1882; LS2029DA1882 ADC to Shafter, Fort Grant, July 9, 1882; LS2036DA1882 ADC to Mason, Fort Verde, July 10, 1882; LS2046DA1882 Willcox to Mackenzie, Santa Fe, July 11, 1882; LS2040DA1882 Willcox to AAG, Military Division of the Pacific, July 15, 1882; LS2102DA1882 Willcox to Military Division of the Pacific, July 18, 1882; LS2120DA1882 Willcox to AAG, Military Division of the Pacific, July 19, 1882, etc.

[10] LS2556DA1882 Willcox to AG, Army, Washington, September 4, 1882.

during the Big Dry Wash outbreak, those were the only civilian casualties during that period.

The troops suffered one soldier and one scout killed, two officers, five soldiers, and one scout wounded, in the battle. Captain Chaffee, in command of the action, won congratulations all around. It was an efficient, workmanlike job. But the campaign and the uproar accompanying it, finally convinced Sherman that it was time for a change in the command of the Department of Arizona, and to find a new man he turned to one of vast Apache experience, Brigadier General George Crook, then commanding the Department of the Platte.

Willcox had not been a bad commander, but he had lacked the rare touch and that appreciation of the hostile mind, along with the vision and decisiveness of command that was needed to solve the Indian problem. Crook possessed these qualities.

Colonel Willcox was informed of the transfer (he was sent to Madison Barracks, New York, where he remained until his retirement in 1886). He complained of a news dispatch which alleged that it was because "affairs in Arizona have been in a very bad condition for the past year, and the Department [of War] has come to the conclusion to make an improvement there," explaining further that Secretary of War Robert Todd Lincoln "was determined to stop the Apache raids and disorders in that Territory and to send an experienced and energetic officer to do the duty."

Willcox charged that Lincoln had spoken

> under a decided misunderstanding of the facts . . . and the difficulties against which I have contended. . . .
>
> Had my recommendations to have a Military Agent placed at San Carlos and my urgent request to have the Cibicu prisoners sent away . . . been granted, I do not believe any further troubles would have happened on the Reservation. The Chiricahua raid

101

was not made across my part of the Mexican border. The Cibicu and Chiricahua campaigns would have been more successful if my orders had been obeyed. The subsequent outbreaks were quickly and effectively punished by troops, partly or wholly under my orders.[11]

His protests, however, were not heeded, and the orders for the transfer stood. Crook took over command of the department on September 4, 1882.

[11] LS2152DA1882 Willcox to AG, Army, Washington, July 21, 1882.

X   CROOK SEEKS THE ANSWER

"The undersigned hereby assumes command of this department," Crook announced, September 4, by means of General
Orders 42 of the Department of Arizona. He immediately
messaged the commander of the Division of the Pacific, at
San Francisco, that "it is very important that the number of
Indian scouts be increased to two hundred and fifty [double
the existing figure]. I should have authority . . . for this increase at once."[1]

That same day he also ordered Company E, Indian Scouts,
"with its pack train," accompanied by a troop of cavalry to
Fort Verde from McDowell to await him on his first tour of
the department.[2] Crook was losing no time. His initial interests, according to the record which has come down to us, concerned his two principal preoccupations during his frontier
service: the Indian scouts and the pack trains, in that order.
On them he depended for the means of carrying on his pe-
culiarly distinctive and effective mode of operations. He en-

[1] LS2552DA1882 Crook to AAG, Military Division of the Pacific, September 4, 1882.
[2] LS2551DA1882 Martin to C.O., Fort McDowell, September 4, 1882.

larged on these matters two days later in a "primer" on Apache warfare which he sent as a message to San Francisco.

> The great difficulty in the solution of the Apache problem is in catching the Indians, which, if done at all, must be mainly through their own people. . . .
> I leave in a day or so to go amongst these Indians, and it may be some weeks before I shall again be within reach of communications, and it is important that I should have that authority [to double the number of his scouts] before I leave here. . . . A well organized pack train is a necessity in operating in this rough country. The pack train here is in such a condition as to need a thorough reorganization. . . .[3]

In appearance George Crook was "manly and strong." This description comes from Crook's loyal aide and longtime admirer, Captain John G. Bourke, an intellectual who found his many years of arduous and interesting work among Indians with the general mentally stimulating and unendingly rewarding to his finely honed ethnological instincts.

Crook, he reported, "was a little over six feet in height, straight as a lance, broad and square-shouldered, full-chested, and with an elasticity and sinewiness of limb which betrayed the latent muscular power gained by years of constant exercise in the hills and mountains of the remoter West."

The commanding officer, said Bourke, had an "ability to learn all that his informant had to supply," and "refused himself to no one, no matter how humble, but was possessed of a certain dignity which repressed any approach to undue familiarity." According to Bourke, Crook "never consulted with any one; made his own plans after the most studious deliberation, and kept them to himself with a taciturnity which

[3] LS2584DA1882 Crook to AAG, Military Division of the Pacific, September 6, 1882.

at times must have been exasperating to his subordinates" (Bourke was one for a long time). Although Crook was "reticent, and secretive, moroseness formed no part of his nature, which was genial and sunny." He was ever interested in the progress and plans of his subordinates even if sometimes testy with his superiors.

"Crook was a man who never indulged in stimulant of any kind—not so much as tea or coffee—never used tobacco, and was never heard to employ a profane or obscene word. . . . No officer could claim that he was ever ordered to do a duty when [Crook] was present, which the latter would not in person lead. No officer of the same rank . . . issued so few orders. According to his creed, officers did not need to be deviled with orders and instructions and memoranda; all that they required was to obtain an insight into what was desired of them."[4]

The difference in orders emanating from the three principal commanding officers during the period discussed in this work was marked. Mackenzie's were terse, clear, and direct. No subordinate could mistake them, or fail to comprehend the commanding officer's wishes, and he knew he had better not fail to carry them out, without sufficient cause.

Willcox had been at various times an attorney in private life, and he sometimes sounded like it in his communications to his subordinates and superiors. A conscientious officer, and thoroughly honest, Willcox tended to worry and, when he did, he became verbose and sometimes confusing. This happened particularly when the going became rough. At such times he would file wordy, sometimes ambiguous orders to junior officers on a scene of action remote from him. He followed these nervously with further orders or suggestions that seemed

[4] Bourke, *On the Border with Crook*, 109–10.

to conflict with previous ones, leaving a field commander occasionally uncertain of what he was expected to do or what his precise instructions were. Sometimes his orders overlapped those of other commanders, as we have seen.

Crook, on the other hand, made it a practice to know his junior officers thoroughly, to trust the good ones completely, to give general directives making clear his intent and purpose, and then to let them have their heads, each to "report personally to me" without regard for chains of command or official channels. His subsequent directions to them, some of which have been preserved, often are in the form of rather fatherly letters of advice, instructions, and suggestions, unmilitary enough, but clearly expressed as though he were taking them into his confidence, which he never, in fact, did.

General Crook concluded the initial phase of his inspection trip in about two weeks. He then messaged San Francisco:

> I have had talks with all the disaffected Indians and arrived at a thorough understanding with them; there is not now a hostile Apache in Arizona. The only band from which we have to fear any trouble is that of the Chiricahuas, now in Mexico, but likely to cross the line at any moment and commit depredations which it will be impossible under present circumstances wholly to prevent, even were we to station our entire army along the border.[5]

He promised fuller particulars by mail, and the next day wrote at length.

The Indians, he had discovered,

> are so firmly of the belief that the affair of the Cibicu last year was an attack premeditated by the white soldiers, that I am convinced any attempt to punish any of the Indian soldiers

[5] LS2784DA1882 Crook to AAG, Military Division of the Pacific, September 27, 1882.

[scouts] for participation in it would bring on war. . . . If the Indians had been in earnest, not one of our soldiers could have gotten away from there alive.

He said that the Indians, at first distrustful and sullen, at last had been persuaded to talk with him, and

they all agreed that affairs could not well be worse. . . . The interpreters were incompetent [no more is heard of Hurrle, or the others] and some of them prejudiced and probably as a consequence of this incompetency and prejudice innocent Indians had been ironed and put in the Guard house. No one knew when his turn would come and they were fast arriving at the conclusion that they were all to be killed anyhow, and they might as well die fighting . . . I have but very little doubt that in a short time there would have been a general outbreak. . . .

Furthermore, I became satisfied . . . that all the troubles of the past season, terminating in the engagement on the summit of Black Mesa in July last [the Battle of Big Dry Wash], were but an outgrowth or culmination of the ill feeling engendered at the Cibicu.

Crook noted that the Mexicans "do not seem to be making much headway" against the wild Chiricahuas in the Sierra Madre. He doubted that pursuit by American troops under the recent convention permitting the crossing of the frontier would have much better results because "we can only follow Indians on hot trails, whereas to ensure success campaigning against them must be incessant."[6]

Having stated the case as he saw it, tracing the ultimate source of the unrest all of the way back to the Cibecue incident and laying the groundwork for his ultimate expedition

[6] Crook to AAG, Military Division of the Pacific, September 28, 1882, Hayes Collection.

into Old Mexico, Crook now turned single-mindedly toward solving the situation, step by step.

The first prerequisite was accurate information of the number of hostiles, their locations, their dispositions, and the chances of weaning any of them from the old, free life to an easier, if perplexing, existence upon a reservation. To do this, Crook organized certain "spy parties," which he sent into Mexico. There is little surviving evidence of the precise nature of these parties, although from the record one can elicit certain clues. In a letter of March 28, 1883, to the assistant adjutant general at San Francisco, Crook admitted that he had sent one party into Mexico soon after his arrival in the department, but "the Mexicans were having a revolution that week and altho' my spies carefully searched the customary haunts of the Chiricahuas, they came upon no trace of them." Later he sent another group down, he said, but although they "found a couple of the Chiricahuas, they were so hostile that my messengers did not dare go any further." He left Captain Emmet Crawford, 3d Cavalry, on the border, with instructions to continue the spy campaign. The captain sent emissaries to near Corralitos and near Casas Grandes, "where they report having seen the Mexican troops but no trace of the hostiles."[7]

Although the personnel of these spy parties is not certain, hints are included among the records of the department. For example, in mid-October, 1882, Crook sent out a party composed entirely of Indians on a mysterious errand. He messaged the commanding officer at Camp Price, the former Camp Supply, at the southern end of the Chiricahua Mountains just north of the line, concerning this group. With this

[7] Crook to AAG, Military Division of the Pacific, March 28, 1883, Hayes Collection.

party of Indians, the messages indicate, Crook had considerable difficulty.

He ordered the commandant to be prepared to ration the party "during the time they may be in that vicinity, say for 25 or 30 days." He had ordered the commanding officer at Fort Thomas (previously Camp Thomas) "to furnish one (1) intelligent n.c. officer and five (5) men—mounted—to accompany 'Navajo Bill' and party of friendly Apaches to Camp Price, where the escort will remain until the Indians shall be ready to return to this post. The n.c.o. will be instructed to communicate by courier . . . the success attending the efforts of 'Navajo Bill' and those with him."

But the closer Navajo Bill got to the jumping-off place, the more reluctant he apparently became. For one thing he was worried about his father-in-law for some reason; Bourke solved that difficulty. Then his ponies played out, he said. Bourke, aide-de-camp to the general, told him by telegraph "he had better go ahead on foot," in that case. The next day Bourke sent another prodding message to Fort Bowie, where Navajo Bill was bogged down: "You will also tell 'Navajo Bill' that Genl. Crook is very much annoyed by his behavior and is tired of hearing about his played out ponies. If his mount is unserviceable he can abandon it and go on foot." The next day Bourke followed that up with another message, "Genl. Crook wishes you to intimate to 'Navajo Bill', without disclosing source of information, that Indians here [at San Carlos] attribute daily count now going on to his dilatoriness in performing his mission and if he and those with him dont exert themselves to the utmost, they'll likely to find themselves in hot water with their own people upon their return."

A description of what may well have been the scouting trip these Indians undertook was told by a participant many

109

years later. An officer mentioned, but not named, would have been Crawford, and the mountain ranges cited are identifiable for the most part: Sierra Espuela, Sierra Enmedio, and so on. The Indian party apparently got no farther south than just below Enmedio, but sent their women on to Carretas, eighteen miles northeast of Bavispe on the road to Janos, the northern fringe of the territory normally "patrolled" by the Sierra Madre hostiles.[8]

By mid-November the Indians were back in Arizona. Bourke messaged Rafferty at Fort Bowie to provide an escort for them to Fort Thomas "from which point Indians can come here alone."[9]

Late in October, Crook reported from San Carlos on what evidently was a second spy party, "Zeiber [Al Sieber] with Apache trailers will leave here in the morning. Indians evince reluctance to performance of [this] duty, alleging that they have on previous occasions been fooled about rewards offered." He urged United States Marshal Z. L. Tidball and United States District Attorney J. W. Zabriskie at Tucson "to see that they receive their just dues as you may have need of their services on similar occasions."[10] In a related message Sieber was authorized to receipt for forage for the five animals of his party, indicating that he was accompanied by

[8] "Experiences of an Indian Scout: Excerpts from the life of John Rope, an 'Old Timer' of the White Mountain Apaches (as told to Grenville Goodwin), Part II," *Arizona Historical Review*, Vol. VII, No. 2 (April, 1936), 51–54.

[9] See LS2935DA1882 Bourke to C.O., Fort Thomas; 2941 Bourke to Scholingen, Willcox; 2942 Bourke to Scholingen; 2944 Bourke to C.O., Fort Bowie; 2948 Bourke to C.O., Fort Bowie; 2985 Bourke to Rafferty, Fort Bowie; 2987 Bourke to Rafferty, Fort Bowie; 2988 Bourke to Rafferty, Fort Bowie; 3070 Bourke to Rafferty, Fort Bowie, all in October and November, 1882, for messages concerned with this expedition.

[10] LS3014DA1882 Crook to Tidball or Zabriskie, Tucson, October 30, 1882.

four Indians, "while in the execution of the duty to which you are now assigned."[11]

The nature of the information brought back by the Navajo Bill and Sieber parties is not now known, beyond Crook's communication of March 28. It is not even certain which party ran into the revolution and which into the hostiles. It is probable that similar groups were dispatched from time to time, if not by Crook directly, then by Crawford.

Late in October the Atchison, Topeka and Santa Fe's affiliate, the Sonora Railway Company Ltd., had completed a line from Guaymas northward through Hermosillo to Nogales, connecting there with a branch to Benson, on the main transcontinental line. Crook was invited to accompany the "excursion party" making the inaugural trip to the Gulf of California on this line on October 25. He was forced to decline, but used the occasion to write young Brigadier General Bernardo Reyes, then just thirty-two, commanding Mexican troops at Hermosillo, expressing regret that he could not have joined the party and met "yourself and your officers, and exchanged views with you upon the Indian question." He added, "I feel sanguine that by harmoniously working together we can soon reduce the last hostile Apache to submission."[12]

To keep things stirred up there were the usual reports, almost invariably false, of Indian depredations and activity at various ranches and through the countryside. One report in early December from Eagle Creek ranchers in eastern Arizona was most circumstantial, reporting "Indians seen on different high points, smoke in deep cañons, cattle killed in different places, moccasins and bare foot tracks around them."

[11] LS3015DA1882 Bourke to Al Zeiber, San Carlos, October 31, 1882.
[12] LS3124DA1882 Crook to Reyes, Hermosillo, November 14, 1882.

Like other such reports they were figments of someone's over-active imagination or were inventions to suit some white rancher's obscure purposes.[13] Crook wrote at length to one such rancher, who had demanded troops near enough to his place to afford "protection" and no doubt incidentally to serve as a market for some of his produce.

> I sympathize fully with your desire to be protected against incursions from hostile Apaches and only regret that the small force of troops under my command renders it impossible to station a detachment at every settlement. You should remember that your case is not an exceptional one; there are hundreds of settlers in precisely the same position and were I to attempt to distribute soldiers at every point where their presence would be in demand, the effective strength of the whole organization would be destroyed.[14]

Rumors from Mexico reported an occasional action against the Chiricahuas, but they were considered more rumor than fact and, although read with interest, were beyond the range of the department's authority or information. However, Crook warned Crawford to "keep a sharp lookout for [the hostiles, should they be driven toward him] and deal them a death blow if possible."[15]

In a detailed communication in early March, 1883, Crook replied to allegations from Mexican Ambassador Extraordinary Matías Romero, through the State Department, that the hostile Apaches were in constant communication with others on the San Carlos Reservation and continued to draw recruits and support from Apaches on that reserve.

[13] LS3189DA1882 Martin to C.O., Fort Thomas, December 11, 1882.
[14] LS100DA1883 Crook to A. C. Richards, near Tombstone, January 29, 1883.
[15] LS182DA1883 Martin to C.O., Fort Bowie, February 15, 1883.

"The Indians committing the outrages from time to time reported in Sonora and Chihuahua, are a band known as the Chiricahuas, who, under their leaders, Ju and Hieronymo, broke out from the San Carlos reservation in April last," before he had reassumed control of the department, he was careful to add, and of a band of Indians that, because of their treaty with Major General Oliver Otis Howard in 1872, had never been under Crook's control, a situation he had long predicted would continue to prove unfortunate.

Crook described his efforts to control the Apaches of Arizona, and to learn of any evasions of that control through the use of informants and in other ways. He continued:

> An occasional spy may possibly get through from the Chiricahuas to the Apaches at the Agency, but spies might get into the City of Mexico. They could not be kept out of the city of Washington during the War, notwithstanding we had at least 100,000 men whose business it was to catch them and hang them if caught. But, I assert that our organization at San Carlos is now so perfect that not an Indian man, woman, or child, can leave there without our knowing it almost before they reach the Gila river.

He charged that rumors, such as those relayed by the Mexican official, originated with "jackals, preying upon human flesh and making a pittance from wars and rumors of war. Peace is abhorrent to their ghoulish natures and if they cannot have a genuine Indian outbreak, they can at least start baseless reports of Indian outrages."

Crook said that his relations with Mexican Army authorities were

> the friendliest and most cordial [and] nothing would give me greater pleasure than to cooperate or combine . . . in operations

to force into submission the persistently hostile Chiricahua Apaches, but the convention recently made with the Mexican Government is so defective that it amounts to nothing.

If the two governments desire the destruction of the Indians who have occasioned so much trouble, I would simply request permission to cross the border. . . . This constant menace to the happiness and prosperity of two communities could be removed at once, and forever.[16]

The reason Crook felt that the "hot pursuit" convention permitting limited crossing of the line was worthless was because of his awareness of the geography of northern Mexico and of the necessity for a carefully planned, thorough, persistent, and perhaps lengthy military operation to produce results. A "hot pursuit" such as was envisioned by the convention, in its literal sense, would have provided for no more than a rushing southward upon the trail of some elusive raiding party. It would be like chasing ghosts or the wind itself, destructive of men and animals and unproductive of any decisive or worthwhile results.

Crook knew the Sierra Madre was a broad and deep mountain region, with peaks not too high, but soaring to nine or ten thousand feet even so. The interior was a labyrinth of uncharted, unexplored, and even unknown canyons, forests, defiles, gorges, and retreats, into which no white man was ever reported to have penetrated, familiar only to the Indians, some of whom, it is rumored, lurk there to this day.

The western side is precipitous. The eastern portion of these north–south mountains is a slanted plateau, rising toward the west, forested, and relatively level until it gets well

[16] LS238DA1883 Crook to AAG, Military Division of the Pacific, March 7, 1883.

into the range, when it breaks off into the jumbled interior of the mass. It is as though a huge wrinkle developed on the earth's surface, bending sheets of rock upward into a giant fold. Over eons of time, the arch of the wrinkle was worn away by water, wind, and time, and the packed formations tilted upright were eaten away to varying degrees, depending upon the resistance of the types of rock which composed them. The result is an interior fearfully rough and varied, a mass of ridges, gorges, bald rock, timbered recesses, and barren knobs, like the bared skeletons of dead animals. And that is exactly what has happened in the manufacture of this mother range of northern Mexico.

Within this range a military task force would be unlikely even to find the enemy without expert guides and the time necessary to work out trails and investigate rumors and clues. Here it would be next to impossible to ambush or entrap any important numbers of Indians, yet necessary to contact and negotiate with them in order to persuade them to give up their free life for the confined and listless life on the reservations. This would be a herculean task under the best of circumstances. Without freedom from such artificial restraints as those posed by the convention, if interpreted literally, it would be hopeless. This was the basis for Crook's persistent grumbling about the convention and his intense dissatisfaction with it.

Throughout his career Crook was a bulldog for information. He felt that a commander without a clear concept of the geography and allied subjects, as well as of the military situation, was at least partially blind.

There occurred about this time, in late March, 1883, another whirlwind raid north of the border, led by a brilliant

115

young Apache war leader, Chatto, or perhaps by Chihuahua, a persistently hostile, yet pragmatic and sensible Indian who had fought so valiantly against García on Aliso Creek.[17]

Although some men were slain by the raiders in Mexico before they reached the line, the Chatto band first came to American military attention with the killing of four men near a charcoal camp on March 21 in the vicinity of Charleston, about ten miles southwest of Tombstone. The inevitable pursuit continued through four hundred miles of the Southwest in which the raiders slew at least twenty-six whites. Among those killed were Federal Judge and Mrs. H. C. McComas, between Silver City and Lordsburg, New Mexico. Their six-year-old son, Charlie, was taken captive. He became the subject of an intense search and much investigation, but was never found.[18]

General Crook reported to the secretary of the interior on March 26:

> The outrages just reported have been committed by a small raiding party of the Chiricahua Apaches, coming back from Mexico. . . . Ten years ago when the other Apache bands were whipped on to the Reservation, the Chiricahuas were specially exempted by the Government from this same subjugation. Since then it is believed that they have killed not less than one thou-

[17] Eve Ball of Hollywood, N.M., an exceptionally able researcher among many of the Chiricahuas descended from this band of hostiles, and an able historical writer, believes from her interviews that Chihuahua was the real leader and Chatto a subleader of this raiding party. Correspondence with author. Contemporary Indian testimony, however, indicates the party was known as "Chatto's band," among at least some other Apaches, and that Chatto was the actual leader of it. But the case is not proved, either way.

[18] A heavy flurry of dispatches in the Letters Received file from the Department of Arizona concern this brief raid, see 307–12; 317–19; 322; and 323 as samples. The exploit has frequently been described, see Thrapp, *Conquest of Apacheria*, 267–73.

sand (1,000) persons in this country and in Mexico. They are constantly trying to stir up mischief among the Agency Indians and so long as they can run back and forth across the border this Territory and New Mexico must look out for trouble. They are the worst band of Indians in America.[19]

[19] LS346DA1883 Crook to Secretary of Interior, Washington, D.C., March 26, 1883.

XI CROOK SOUNDS THE MEXICANS

In order to carry out the plan, then developing in his mind, of plunging into the Sierra Madre with a sufficient force to overawe the hostiles, Crook needed several things. First, he needed the excuse of a raid or something similar which might qualify his expedition as "hot pursuit," in the event of anyone overly curious; second, precise information about the enemy's location and, if possible, a trustworthy guide; third, the assurance of co-operation, or at least noninterference, by Mexican army and government officials; and, fourth, permission from his own superiors.

The Chatto raid provided him with the first of these prerequisites. Surprisingly, from the raiding party he also got the second. For the third, he must make two trips into Mexico in person, and these he now prepared himself to undertake.

Late in March Crook messaged Second Lieutenant Britton Davis at San Carlos that the raiders were headed toward that place, "possibly some squaws with them," and urged the officer to send out scouts "to try to capture a squaw for information."[1] Davis did better. He had established a useful network of spy-informants among the Indians at San Carlos,

[1] LS363DA1883 Martin to Davis, San Carlos, March 27, 1883.

and on April 1 could inform the general by telegraph: "Excitement last night was caused by one Chiricahua. I captured him at sun-rise this morning in Nodeski's camp, twelve miles from here. . . . No other hostiles around camp so far as can learn. Prisoner surrendered without making attempt to escape or resistance. Was not shot at."[2] For good measure, he also arrested Nodeski, charging him with harboring renegades. Nodeski was sent to Fort Thomas in irons, with the recommendation that he be dispatched to the Dry Tortugas, preferably for life.[3] A minor chief, Nodeski seems often to have been implicated by hostiles in their actions, although there is no proof that he ever went out himself. Davis had ironed him because the captured Chiricahua had made for his camp and presumably was sheltered there. Nodeski was confined for about six months, then released "pretty well broke up" and promising never to cause any trouble in the future. He had been implicated in the Cibecue incident and within a couple of years would be involved in the Geronimo breakout. Nodeski apparently was incorrigible.[4]

The captured Chiricahua, whose name was Pah-na-yo-tishn, the "Coyote Saw Him," or Tsoe, was nicknamed Peaches by white soldiers because of his complexion. He became celebrated as Crook's master guide into the Sierra Madre. The general interviewed him at length at Willcox. Antonio Diaz, a twelve-year captive of the Apaches, inter-

[2] John G. Bourke Diary, April 1, 1883, LXIV, 67–68. Hereafter cited as Bourke, Diary.

[3] P. P. Wilcox to Interior Secretary H. M. Teller, April 1, 1883, printed textually in *New York Herald*, April 2, 1883.

[4] See AT9949WD1881 Tiffany to Commissioner Indian Affairs, September 25, 1881; Crawford to Crook, November 1, 1883, Hayes Collection; Crawford to Crook, November 14, 1883, Hayes Collection; Crook to Crawford, November 14, 1885, Hayes Collection.

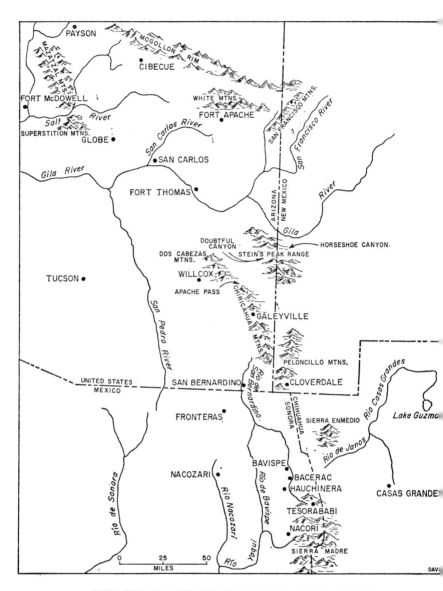

THEATER OF OPERATIONS OF THE SIERRA MADRE
EXPEDITION

preted from Apache into Spanish, and Captain Bourke and Ramon Montoya, a nephew of Diaz's, from Spanish to English.[5] Betzinez affirmed that Pah-na-yo-tishn had been a willing member of the raiding party, a good friend of Ben-act-i-ney, who had been killed at the charcoal camp, and had decided later to separate from the raiders and go to San Carlos, having no difficulty in leaving the band.[6] But in his interview with Crook, Peaches, as he hereafter would be known, said that, as a San Carlos Apache, he was a virtual prisoner of the Chiricahuas and had accompanied them to Mexico under duress because his two wives were Chiricahuas. Both had been slain in the García fight. He was forced to steal away in the night from the raiding party, he said.[7] It is possible that he stressed his reluctance to raid because he feared summary treatment if the white soldiers thought he had been hostile of his own free will. But there is no proof of that, and Betzinez might have been mistaken.[8]

Peaches spoke freely of the Apache "stronghold" in the Sierra Madre and of the life of the hostiles there, their fights with Mexicans, and how the various bands lived. He described Chatto's raid in detail, asserting it had left Mexico with twenty-six men, reduced to twenty-four with the defection of himself and the death of Ben-act-i-ney. From Railroad Pass, between the Pinaleño and Dos Cabezas mountains, the raiders sent two others of their number, Dutchy and Kah-thli, to a well-known former Apache captive, translator, and scout, Merejildo Grijalva, to "find out all you can about the Agency

[5] The full transcript of this interview is in Bourke, Diary, LXV, 20–31.

[6] Betzinez, *I Fought With Geronimo*, 117–18.

[7] Bourke, Diary, LXV, 25–26.

[8] Rope, "Experiences of an Indian Scout," *Arizona Historical Review*, Vol. VII, No. 2 (April, 1936), 51n.

and how the Indians there feel."[9] Merejildo, explained
Peaches, was a relative of these two raiders "because their
people [whom Bourke explained were the clan or gens] raised
him" when he was a captive boy. Ten days later these two
Apaches apparently were persuaded by Merejildo to surrender, after finding him at Safford. Lieutenant Davis ironed
them at San Carlos and sent them to Fort Thomas, where they
were held pending Crook's return from Mexico. To improve
their prospects, no doubt, they reportedly brought an offer
of surrender "of all Chiricahuas." But it was too late, if the
offer was genuine. The general already was well on his way
toward the Sierra Madre.[10]

Peaches said the Chiricahuas had fled the reservation because of being kicked, cuffed around, and generally mistreated
by "that agent with the big stomach [Tiffany]. The Chiricahuas couldn't stand it. They saw he didn't want them on the
Reservation, so they left. Everything that has happened is
on acct. of that agent with the fat stomach. It's all his fault."[11]

The Apache said the hostiles, numbering about seventy
warriors and fifty boys big enough to bear arms and fight,
were well supplied with sixteen-shot rifles, but ammunition
was a problem. "When they left the stronghold they were
much in need of ammunition and they knew that by coming
up to the Line, they'd find people who were well-armed. They
killed those met to get a new supply of cartridges and arms.
They got altogether (8) eight new guns and from each man
killed from 10 to 15 cartridges."[12] He said that food was
scarce in the stronghold, except for meat, but of mescal, the

[9] Bourke, Diary, LXV, 22–23.
[10] LS522DA1883 Martin to Crook, by courier, May 2, 1883.
[11] Bourke, Diary, LXV, 23.
[12] Ibid., 23–24.

yucca-like plant whose starchy core the Apaches loved, there was little, and troops might be able to starve them out if their net was tight enough. Peaches agreed to be a guide for Crook to the Apache stronghold, and the general ordered the prisoner's irons struck off.

Crook believed Peaches was honest and reported truthfully to him and that his capture had been a turning point in his preparations for his major campaign.

Although heavily occupied with the planning and organization of the campaign, Crook took time out some days later to congratulate Lieutenant Davis on effecting the surrender, a gesture typical of Crook and his relations with his subordinates.

He complimented the officer on the

energetic and intelligent manner in which you have administered military affairs at the San Carlos . . . and especially in all relating to the capture of the Chiricahua Apache. . . . The duties devolving upon you have been of an especially delicate nature and in their execution you have won not only the approval of your military superiors, but have also been mentioned in a very flattering manner in a letter received from Agent P. P. Wilcox.[13]

The letter must have set Davis up for days.

To fulfill his third requirement, Crook determined to visit Mexican army officers and others in Sonora, and, upon his return, to visit those in Chihuahua.

On April 8 the general, accompanied by Bourke, his valued aide, and First Lieutenant Gustav Joseph Fiebeger,[14] en-

[13] LS490DA1883 Crook to Davis, San Carlos, April 19, 1883.

[14] Born at Akron, Ohio, May 9, 1858, Fiebeger was graduated from the U.S. Military Academy in 1879 and became a distinguished military civil engineer, serving in many capacities. He died October 18, 1939. *Who Was Who.*

gineer officer of the department, left for Guaymas over the new Sonora Railway Company line.[15] They arrived the following day, putting up at the Hotel Cosmopolitan. General Topete, his young face scarred by a machete in a revolutionary action some years previously, greeted Crook warmly. On April 10 the American had a formal interview with Topete and his superior, Major General Carbo.

Crook explained what Peaches had told him about the stronghold and the Apache manner of living there, then said that "he had determined to put an end to the Apache atrocities, to do which would require the co-operation of the Mexican forces; that the convention now existing . . . was too indefinite and would cause failure to follow upon any plans limited by its provisions." General Topete and General Carbo (Bourke described the latter as "a dignified, intellectual man" wearing a "rich, emerald-green satin sash" under his coat to proclaim his rank) sympathized, but said it was beyond their authority to grant privileges not specified by the convention. This might have dashed Crook's hopes for a dramatic end to the Apache campaigning, except that Carbo quickly added that he recognized "the imperfections of the present agreement which might frustrate operations." He would, he said, do "all in his power to aid in their subjugation," and while he could not grant permission to Crook to go after the hostiles "without regard to trails," yet, he slyly added, "he would interpose no objection, provided his government made none."

Carbo further suggested that both sides petition their governments for modifications in the convention, but knowingly added that "should General Crook find it necessary to cross

---

[15] Bourke, Diary, LXV, 36–96; LXVI, 1–17, covers these trips in detail and apparently is the only source that does.

the Border before these changes had been perfected, he wished him to have his Indian allies wear a distinctive badge" and notify General Topete, in charge of Apache operations in Sonora.

This was far better than Crook had hoped. He said his Apache scouts would wear a red headband, which they ever afterward did.[16] The interview broke up joyously with "refreshments including Champaign, sherry, mescal, brandy and beer." Before his hosts could change their minds, Crook hustled his party aboard the train and pulled out for Arizona.

On April 13, Crook left for Chihuahua. They spent the first night at El Paso, in "the miserable parody upon an inn known as the Central Hotel," according to Bourke, and crossed the line the next day, reaching Chihuahua at sunset. Interviews were held with Mayor Juan Zubiran and Brigadier General Ramon Raguero who, noted Bourke, "cannot be compared to either [Carbo or Topete] in brain power." An understanding was reached resembling the earlier one. Crook also met Governor Mariano Samaniego and Colonel Terrazas. This might have been Joaquin Terrazas, destroyer of Victorio, rather than Luis Terrazas, former governor and a key figure in northern Mexico, for Luis then held the rank of general, while Joaquin, his cousin, never rose above colonel, Crook, however, referred to his conversation with "Governors Samaniego and Terrazas," which implied that it was with Luis.[17]

The return to the United States was made April 16.

On leaving Whipple Barracks early that month to visit the southern part of the territory (a circuitous route through

---

[16] Rope, "Experiences of an Indian Scout," *Arizona Historical Review*, Vol. VII, No. 2 (April, 1936), 55.

[17] Crook, *Annual Report*, 1883, Appendix E, Hayes Collection.

New Mexico was necessary if one wished to go by rail), Crook had conferred on April 4 with Mackenzie at Albuquerque regarding his Mexico plans. Now, on the sixteenth, he telegraphed Mackenzie in reply to a request for a second meeting, saying they might confer at Deming. In transit, however, an error was made, the telegram reporting he would leave the "morning of the 18th," instead of the sixteenth, and Mackenzie missed him. In wiring explanations, Mackenzie said "I do not wish you to start without knowing that my not seeing you was due to an error . . . and that I have every wish to 'hold up your hands' in your difficult undertaking."[18]

An additional boost was given by Matías Romero, who, aware of the unlikelihood of positive action by the Mexican government and also aware of the need for Crook's expedition and its success, said that he had been importuned by Secretary of State Frederick T. Frelinghuysen and accordingly had telegraphed his government.

> As telegraphing was, however, an unsatisfactory method of communication upon such subjects, he [Romero] proposed, he said, to forward an official letter by mail. . . . He said he did not believe there would be time to accomplish anything in relation to this particular case at the present session of the Senate, which would expire in the latter part of May, as his official letter would not reach Mexico for two or three weeks, and it would be some time after that before the subject could be laid before the Senate officially.

Thus, Romero put no obstacles in Crook's path, and he saw to it that his government would not have time to do so officially, either.[19]

For his fourth prerequisite, Crook had a March 31 dispatch

[18] LS127DNM1883 Mackenzie to Crook, April 25, 1883.
[19] *New York Herald*, April 30, 1883.

from General of the Army Sherman authorizing him "under existing orders to destroy hostile Apaches, to pursue them regardless of department or national lines, and to proceed to such points as you deem advisable."[20] Although this dispatch was sent him at the height of the Chatto uproar, it seemed to supply the necessary permission. On April 18, in accordance with his understanding with Carbo and Raguero, Crook wired the adjutant general urging "immediate steps" to correct the convention.[21] To this Sherman hastily replied that "negotiations for modifying now going on with Mexican Government but it cannot be inferred that Gov't. will assent to any modification," and the secretary of war instructed Crook that "*no* military movements must be made into, or within the Territory of Mexico, which is not authorized."[22]

Crook acknowledged receipt and protested that "it is not my intention to violate convention between the two governments." He would start immediately, he said, "in pursuit of the savages in accordance with the treaty."[23]

Added to the very real perils and physical risks of his unorthodox and imaginative expedition, Crook now had added the equally genuine risk to his own career if he failed, or if the Mexicans changed their minds and decided to create difficulties for him. Any way the situation might be examined, Crook was a man on a limb, sawing furiously and hoping to get back successfully before the limb fell. But Crook was a man to take such risks, and, more frequently than not, he carried them off.

In this case the die was cast.

[20] Schofield to Crook, March 31, 1883, Crook, *Annual Report*, 1883, Appendix D, Hayes Collection.
[21] Crook to AG, Washington, D.C., April 18, 1883, Hayes Collection.
[22] Sherman to Crook, April 28, 1883, Hayes Collection.
[23] Crook to AG, Washington, D.C., April 30, 1883, Hayes Collection.

XII THE PLUNGE SOUTHWARD

Leaving a screen of troops to protect the border and prevent, if possible, hostile raiding parties from crossing it, Crook prepared to plunge south of the line on May 1. His expeditionary force consisted of 193 Apache scouts, commanded by Captain Emmet Crawford and assisted by Second Lieutenant Charles B. Gatewood, 6th Cavalry, and Second Lieutenant James O. Mackay, 3d Cavalry. Al Sieber was chief of scouts and Archie McIntosh and Sam Bowman were his assistants. Mickey Free and Severiano were interpreters.

Captain Chaffee commanded a forty-two–man company of the 6th Cavalry, assisted by First Lieutenant Frank West and Second Lieutenant William Woods Forsyth. Acting Assistant Surgeon George Andrews was assisted by hospital steward J. B. Sweeney. Crook's staff included Captain Bourke and Lieutenant Fiebeger. The pack train was made up of various units; a total of 266 mules; and seventy-six packers, who were civilians, half Mexicans and half Anglos. If Tom Horn accompanied the expedition, he did so as an ordinary packer.

Prior to the expedition, the Apaches who intended to accompany Crook on the campaign built themselves up for the expedition, in part by war dances. Nevertheless, enthusiasm for the expedition was not universal among them. One Indian, saying "he had nothing against" the enemy down there, refused to go and was derided by his companions. He evidently was an exception.[1]

The force, as finally composed, "was the maximum which could be supplied by the use of every available pack animal in the Department, and the minimum with which I could hope to be successful in the undertaking," reported Crook. "We had supplies, field rations, for sixty days, and one hundred and fifty rounds of ammunition to the man. To reduce baggage, officers and men carried only such clothing and bedding as was absolutely necessary, and instead of keeping up their own messes, the officers shared the food of the packers."[2]

"The entire command," wrote one participant, "felt that they were going on a perilous expedition, but they had faith in their commander."[3]

John Rope reported that before the departure "a big meeting was held" with Crook, his officers, and the scouts, several of the scout sergeants doing the talking for the Indians. He reported Crook as asking:

"What do you scouts think about us catching the Chiricahuas down in Mexico, do you think we will find them?"

A San Carlos sergeant named Tu-is-ba replied that "we could never catch the Chiricahuas because they could hide like coyotes and smell danger a long way like wild animals."

Crook replied: "I think we are going to catch these Chiri-

[1] Opler, An Apache Life-Way, 339.

[2] Crook, Annual Report for 1883, Appendix E.

[3] Diarist, May 1, 1883. An unsigned diary of the expedition, printed in the Arizona Star June 17, 1883, is used here as "Diarist." It probably was kept by Lieutenant Forsyth, see James H. McClintock, Arizona: Prehistoric, Aboriginal, Pioneer, Modern, I, 246. Also used is John G. Bourke's Diary, and Crook's Annual Report, 1883, op. cit.

cahuas, and we are going to keep after them till we catch them all. We have orders from Washington, where the President lives, to catch these Chiricahuas. We are all wearing his clothes and eating his grub, and so I want you to help him. In this way we can repay him." He then promised the scouts that the government would reward them. Rope went on:

"I think [Crook] was telling us the truth all right, because all of us scouts are now drawing pensions." The general advised his scouts to put on a big war dance, and they would leave the following morning.[4]

In his *Annual Report* for 1883 Crook summarized the vast difficulties of campaigning after Apaches and of fighting them.

An Indian in his mode of warfare is more than the equal of the white man, and it would be practically impossible with white soldiers to subdue the Chiricahuas in their own haunts. The country they inhabit is larger than New England, and the roughest on the continent, and though affording no food upon which soldiers can subsist, provides the Indian with everything necessary for sustaining his life indefinitely. The agave grows luxuriantly in all their mountains, and upon this plant alone the Indians can live. They have no property . . . nor settled habitations of any kind, but roam about like coyotes, and their temporary resting places are chosen with all the experience gained by generations of warfare. The Indian knows every foot of his territory; can endure fatigue and fasting, and can live without food or water for periods that would kill the hardiest mountaineer. In fighting them we must of necessity be the pursuers, and unless surprised by sudden and unexpected attack, the advantages are all in their favor.

It should be remembered that in Indian combats you rarely see an Indian, you see the puff of smoke and hear the whiz of his

[4] Rope, "Experiences of an Indian Scout," *Arizona Historical Review*, Vol. VII, No. 2 (April, 1936), 55–56.

bullets, but the Indian is thoroughly hidden. The soldier on the contrary must expose himself, since he is the attacking party. In operating against them the only hope of success lies in using their own methods, and their own people with a mixed command. The first great difficulty to be met is to locate them, and this must be done by Indian scouts, then we must move against them in such manner that the Indians may not discover our movements. The marches must be by stealth, and at night. The Indian scouts must be kept sufficiently in advance of the troops to be able to discover the enemy without being seen themselves. . . . They must leave absolutely no trail, but must travel over rocks, and keep constantly under cover. The enemy discovered, runners are sent back to the command, which must make forced night marches, so as to attack by surprise; the scouts meantime if possible surround the hostile camp, and keeping constantly concealed should be able to give all possible information with reference to the situation of the camp. . . .

The Indian's eyes are as keen as the eagle's, and his natural instincts developed to the highest degree. The unusual movement of a bush, the falling of a rock, the glint of the sun from the weapons of the scouts, will immediately send them scudding like a bevy of frightened quail.

The surprise over, the Indians who escape are secure, pursuit is impossible in a country where every rock may hide a fugitive enemy, from behind which with the present improved weapons in his hands, he can kill at will without exposing himself. Nothing can be done except to return to your base, wait until matters have quieted down, and then repeat the operation.[5]

With these principles, already well learned in a hundred small combats, the general and his taut, efficient, but not over-large command, marched across the border from the San Bernardino Ranch[6] and disappeared, so far as his su-

[5] Crook, *Annual Report*, 1883, 11–12.
[6] This noted ranch was almost an army headquarters during Apache war

periors and the United States as a whole were concerned, for forty-one days.

"We moved south-east down the San Bernardino [River], the most northerly branch of the Yaqui, the largest river of western Mexico," reported Crook. "For three days we did not see a human being. The whole country had been laid waste by the Apaches, and much land of value and formerly cultivated, had grown up into a jungle of cane and mesquite. We followed the trail which our guide, 'Peaches,' assured me had been made by the hostile Chiricahuas."

The first day the command marched eighteen miles to the junction of the San Bernardino and an easterly tributary, Elias Creek. "Nothing occurred on the march worthy of mention," reported the diarist. Bourke added, however, that the Apaches that day killed several deer and a "couple of wild turkeys," although some of them were reluctant to eat the latter. Almost as an afterthought he remembered that a rattlesnake, as thick as his wrist, had crawled across the blankets while he and Fiebeger were dozing in camp, and "furnished a source of pleasurable excitement."

All next day they worked south, along the endlessly meandering, but generally south-flowing San Bernardino. The thick jungle of sacaton, cane, willow, and ash was so dense that they could not march in the river bed, but were forced to clamber up and down over the low bluffs to the right of the stream. The scouts blithely kept pace, all the while whittling flutes out of lengths of cane and wondering at the lead-footed whites. After twenty miles, according to the diarist, they camped on the Bavispe. The map of Crook's route, however, shows the camp to have been north of Batepito, described at

times. Of considerable extent, it was bought by the famous John H. Slaughter the year after the Crook Mexico expedition. Barnes, *Place Names*, 380.

that time as a "deserted ranch" (today it is a thriving community, complete with irrigated farmlands and an airplane landing strip).[7] That day Bourke "nearly drowned in a quicksand, after getting lost in a canebrake."

The next day, May 3, they marched twenty miles southeast, making camp where an unnamed tributary joins the Bavispe from the northeast. On the fourth they threaded the canyon of the Bavispe River, working upstream and crossing the water eight times. They camped just above San Miguel (San Miguelito), a river town downstream from the community of Bavispe, founded in the eighteenth century.[8] "Still nothing to indicate the presence of the hostiles," reported the diarist, but Bourke said that the previous day "tracks of hostiles mounted on ponies" were seen, fairly fresh. On May 5, camp was broken nine miles north of Bavispe, and the column marched south, past San Miguel, on the river bluffs west of them. "When we got within sight of Bavispe we stopped," reported Rope. "Sieber ordered a hundred of us scouts to go ahead and the rest to follow. We went on, right through the streets,"[9] the Mexicans silently peering at these Apaches stalking through their very community, under white commanders.

Bavispe, said by Bourke to have been "about 200 years old," was, like Bacerac to the south, actually far older than that. Both were ancient pueblos of the Opata Indians, inveterate enemies of the Apaches. Baptisms were performed at both places about 1610 and intermittently thereafter, and a presidio was established at Bavispe between 1781 and

[7] Paul M. Roca, *Paths of the Padres Through Sonora*, 208–209.

[8] *Ibid.*, 209.

[9] Rope, "Experiences of an Indian Scout," *Arizona Historical Review*, Vol. VII, No. 2 (April, 1936), 57.

1786.[10] The presidio is on a low bluff west of the Bavispe River, where the stream makes a wide sweep to the east, and commands a splendid view up and down the river. It is a natural site for a frontier fort and was the focus for Apache fighting for scores of years. The command, however, continued due south from Bavispe, toward Bacerac, camping just below it on the right bank of the river.

A merchant named Samaniego, delighted to see the American forces, gave Crook a bottle of good brandy as a welcoming present. The general, who rarely used liquor in any form, and never to excess, took it graciously. When the visitor had departed, he dropped it somewhere among his personal duffle where it remained through the events to come, but was not forgotten.

Bourke noted the desolate character of the country, ravished for years by hostile Indians. "All the people in northern Sonora are armed to resist the Apaches," he wrote. "They work in their fields with arms in their hands and have organized into patrols which in bands of 25 or 30 each day explore the country, looking for trails or other signs of the hostiles."[11]

At the Bacerac camp "Sieber and some of the others butchered ten cattle without permission from the Mexicans," reported Rope. "In a little while the mayor of the town, a Mexican, came riding out on a little pony. . . . He talked some time with the officers, and I guess they had to pay him for those ten steers."[12]

---

[10] Roca, *Paths of the Padres Through Sonora*, 212–15.

[11] Bourke, Diary, LXVII, 2.

[12] Rope, "Experiences of an Indian Scout," *Arizona Historical Review*, Vol. VII, No. 2 (April, 1936), 57. Bourke said Crook bought four steers for twenty dollars each, adding that the meat was "stringy and tough." Rope is quite inaccurate on figures, but one assumes that his recollection of basic facts is sound.

Then a celebration began. According to Bourke:

The bells of the church were ringing a mad peal announcing
that to-morrow would be Sunday, when a prolonged thumping
upon a drum gave the signal that a "Baile" was about to commence. Wending our way to the corner from which the noise
proceded, we found that Zeiber, Frank Monach [packer], Hopkins [another packer] and several others had bought out the
whole stock of a "tienda" which seemed to deal only in "mescal,"
Everyone passing along the street was collared and "run in" and
. . . made to take a drink. An orchestra was recruited of a bass
drum, a snare drum and 2 squeaky fiddles to play "for the
drinks." None of them knew a note of music and whenever any
special piece was called for, it was first necessary to whistle the
air which the players readily caught and rendered with enthusiasm emphasized by the 2 drums. This orchestra was augmented after a while by the addition of a man with a sax-horn.
He couldn't play and the horn had lost several keys, but he
added to the noise and was welcomed with screams of applause.
. . . The new player was doing some good work with his horn,
when a couple of dancers whirled into him, knocking him clean
off his pins and astraddle of the bass drum and drummer. Confusion reigned, but only for a moment and good humor was
restored by the liberal administration of mescal.[13]

Bourke noted that "there were many swelled heads among
our packers" the next morning, "but we moved out at an
early hour." Ten miles southward they came to the town of
Huachinera, "300 pop. a squalid hole, with a squalid church."
Others did not share his impression.[14] Huachinera, a compact

[13] Bourke, Diary, LXVII, 7–8.

[14] Roca found the old church "magnificent, with good paintings and excellent altar decorations," but does not give the precise date of its construction,
although believing that it was more than two hundred years old, suggesting
he and Bourke saw the same one. *Paths of the Padres Through Sonora*, 216.

village on a rocky hummock overlooking a creek, tributary to the Bavispe, whose main course here is to the east, has not grown much in the century since Bourke visited it, but at least it has a new church. The community is dominated by a long and massive ridge, heavily forested and nearly seven thousand feet high, to the southeast, the tallest range the expedition had yet encountered as it approached the Sierra Madre.

"Our Chiricahua prisoner says that the Chiricahuas [Chatto's band] came through this place when they started on their raid in March; and he asserts unqualifiedly that (16) sixteen of them entered the plaza of Huachinera in broad daylight and purchased tobacco."[15]

The Crook command camped at some springs near Tesorababi, a ranch which Bourke said had been "abandoned on account of Indian depredations."

Until now the party had traveled along the main trail from Janos through Bavispe toward Oputo. At Tesorababi the main trail struck directly west toward Oputo, another noted Apache-fighting center, thirty miles distant.

In order not to reveal his true intentions to any sharp-eyed sentinels, Crook ordered the command to lay over at Tesorababi all day. Under the cover of darkness they moved out again, heading south a few miles and then southeast into the mountains. Once within the shelter of their folds and wrinkles, Crook could once more move confidently by daylight. While the troops lay about camp near Tesorababi, awaiting nightfall, four Mexicans "riding mules and donkeys came into camp," reported Bourke. "They were coming up from a place called Bacadehuachi," thirty miles south of Oputo, "to Bacerac. From them I learned that Colonel Aguerre was going

15 Bourke, Diary, LXVII, 9.

to-day or to-morrow with (400) four hundred regular troops for a scout in the Sierra Madre and that he would be assisted by all available force of the National Guard of the District of Moctezuma, which, it was expected, would be about (3,000) three thousand strong."[16] So Crook's request for co-operation by Mexican forces was bearing fruit, after all. No more is heard of this expedition, however, and the results, if any, of its operation are unknown.

From here on into the mountains, it is difficult to correlate the various accounts although the best and most reliable is apparently the account by John Bourke. By collating his text with the Crook map, we can arrive at a fairly accurate approximation of where the command went and where it was on a particular day although the lack of dates at camp sites on the chart somewhat limits the precision of this method. The diarist is obscure on this movement, and John Rope is very unclear on how many days were spent on the march or where the command operated. Crook makes no attempt to give a day-by-day record in his *Annual Report*, merely remarking on important incidents or points as they occurred.

Scarcely had the column penetrated the lower skirts of the sierra when the first crisis arose. A. Frank Randall, correspondent-photographer of the *New York Herald*, accompanying the expedition, displayed a young owl, "still in the down," tied to the pommel of his saddle, and the Apaches would have none of it. "They said the owl was a bird of ill-omen, and that we could not hope to whip the Chiricahuas so long as we retained it," wrote Bourke. "The moon-eyed bird of night was set free and the advance resumed."[17]

[16] *Ibid.*, 11–12.
[17] *Ibid.*, 14; John G. Bourke, *An Apache Campaign in the Sierra Madre*, 74. The Apaches' extraordinary fear of owls, which they hold to be a link

From the map, and from aerial photographs of the terrain, it seems evident that Crook went through a saddle on the right of the long upheaval which begins southeast of Huachinera and continues southerly. Then the expedition dropped to the upper Bavispe River, which flows east of the long mountain. This took five days of ferociously difficult movement over trails or semi-trails left by the raiding Chiricahuas and littered with castaway plunder, the bodies of animals, traces of rancherias, and other rubbish the heedless Indians had abandoned.

"The signs of the presence of hostile Chiricahuas became abundant" as they entered the mountains, wrote Crook.

> There were abandoned camps of fifteen, twenty, thirty and forty families; cattle, horses and ponies, living and dead.
>
> The country was the roughest imaginable but well suited as a place of refuge for the Chiricahuas, who, unless taken by sudden surprise, could, from their points of vantage, withstand an army. We found at all times an abundance of the purest water and plenty of fuel, the mountains being covered with forests of pine and oak. We made our way cautiously, and with considerable difficulty, farther and farther into the recesses of the Sierra Madre, the trail becoming very precipitous. A number of mules were lost by slipping over precipices. . . .
>
> On the 12th, the guide "Peaches" conducted us to the stronghold of the enemy, a formidable place, impregnable to attack, had such been dreamed of.

At this time, according to Bourke and the map, the Apaches were encamped in a natural amphitheater on an upper tribu-

---

with ghosts and a decided influence for evil, is described in Opler, *An Apache Life-Way*, 30, 229–31. It is possible that Randall's later misfortune, in losing most of his photographic equipment might have been traced by some superstitious Apache to his handling of the dreaded bird.

tary of the Bavispe, with mountains all around, although the basin they were in was well grassed and wooded.

The whole Sierra Madre is a natural fortress, and to drive the Chiricahuas from which, by any method other than those we employed, would have cost hundreds of lives. The enemy was not to be found in this particular fortress [the stronghold]. The nature of the Apaches impels them to change their camps every few days, and thus avoid as much as possible anything like a surprise. Indeed, they never have anything like a permanent camp. Their temporary abodes are merely brush "wich-a-ups," which can be built in half an hour and destroyed in a few moments, so as to leave to the unpracticed eye hardly a trace of their presence.

On parts of the route, so precipitous and toilsome had become the way, pack mules made barely one mile an hour, Bourke reported. One mule, falling over a precipice to its death, bore most of Randall's photographic apparatus, "which was crushed to smithereens."[18] Bourke added that

the trail from this on was, if anything, more dreadful than it had been yesterday. . . . Up! Up! Up! Perspiration running from every brow, the trail zig-zagging up the vertical or almost vertical slope of a ridge, very nearly a thousand feet above the water. "Look out!" comes the warning cry from those in the lead, and then those in the rear dodge nervously from the trajectory of some piece of rock, which, dislodged by the feet of horses or men has shot downward, gathering momentum each second as if shot from a catapult. To look at this country is grand; to travel in it, is Hell. We are taking the greatest precautions not to be seen and not to be surprised; detachments of scouts cover the country like swarms of locusts.

18 Bourke, Diary, LXVII, 24.

On May 11 Crook held a council of war with his officers and scouts. The scouts told him

> that they hoped to find the Chiricahuas and surround them; that if they had a fight and the Chiricahuas refused to submit, they would kill the last one, and if they did submit they thought that some of the bad ones, like Ju and Hieronymo ought to be put to death anyhow, as they would be all the time raising trouble. General Crook replied that if the Chiricahuas thought proper to fight, they should have all the fighting they wanted and the scouts couldn't kill too many to suit him, but wanted them to save women and children and grant mercy to all who asked for it. . . .
>
> The scouts then organized a scout of (150) one hundred and fifty men under Crawford, Gatewood and Mackay; with them Zeiber, McIntosh, Mickey Free, Severiano and Bowman to examine the country carefully for signs of the hostiles; the pack animals with the Cavalry command, packers and rest of the Apache scouts remaining in this bivouac.[19]

John Rope was a member of this important advance party.[20] He left the only account by a participant.

Crawford, "with the tireless scouts and himself as tireless," went on ahead, reported the diarist.

"I had never fought with the Chiricahua and did not know how mean they were, so I was always in the front," said Rope. "Pretty soon we came to some old tracks. Here the Chiricahuas had left one horse. He was very poor, but we butchered him and took out his liver and meat that was good. . . . We went on ahead to another camp at a canyon near the head of the Bavispe River. . . . We could see where the Chiricahuas

[19] *Ibid.*, 30–31.

[20] Rope, "Experiences of an Indian Scout," *Arizona Historical Review*, Vol. VII, No. 2 (April, 1936), 58.

had been having a dance." One Warm Springs Apache looked at the tracks and said they resembled a war dance. The scouting continued, the scouts searching the surrounding countryside cautiously with binoculars at every opportunity.

Back with the main body, Bourke reported that twenty-five or thirty Mexican packers and half a dozen Indians made an excursion to a most difficult location where there recently had been a savage fight between Mexican troops and Apaches, with uncertain results, depending upon which side told the story.

General Topete had given a preliminary report on this action on May 1. It had commenced when Colonel García, marching from Moctezuma with eighty federal troops and fifty auxiliaries, pursued an Apache band toward the Sierra Madre. After five days the hostiles were located. The attacking force divided into two columns, with García commanding one and Colonel Lorenzo Torres the other. After a fierce fight the enemy was defeated, reported the Mexicans, with eleven killed. García reported three killed and eight wounded among his own men.

On May 12, in possession of more complete information, Topete enlarged on the report. García took up the trail of a band, estimated at 150 Indians, which had been depredating along the frontier. He commanded a column of eighty-six soldiers and fifty auxiliaries. While on the Indians' trail García absorbed Torres' company of auxiliaries as well. They doggedly pursued the Indians. On April 25, after five days of hard marching deep in the Sierra Madre at "a point whose name is unknown," the Indians were located "in two positions in impregnable points and difficult of access." In a graphic description of the difficulties overcome, the report said that García maintained a frontal assault while Torres worked around to the left, the only point of access to the enemy position. After three hours of fighting, from 2 until 5 P.M., the Indians were driven off, leaving eleven dead and with many wounded, "according to the bloody tracks they left." In all, the Mexicans fired 2,876 shots, said the report, and their losses were put at four dead and seven wounded.[21]

Bourke reported that the packers, on their return from the site, had stories that

> varied greatly, no two agreeing; but that the Chiricahuas had given the Mexicans a good drubbing was evidenced. They found (3) three Mexicans buried under piles of rocks—and down in the cañon alongside the battlefield, they claimed to have seen the grave of a dead Chiricahua. There were two (2) parapets of stone and numbers of exploded copper cartridges cal. 50 [used by the Mexicans] and Winchester [the weapon of the Chiricahuas].[22]

The Crook map shows this fight to have occurred on the reverse slope, that is to say, on the eastern slope of the southern tip of the long mountain, although this does not quite square with Bourke's directions. The map location would be two or three miles southwest of the camp, while the captain said it was southeast. It may have been a simple slip or error on his part.

Crawford meanwhile had been working the country on ahead, as thoroughly as possible. On May 14 he sent back a note to Crook:

[21] 114814/12221, 1883, Cuaderno 12, Secretario de Guerra y Marina. Partes de novedades relativos a asesinatos cometidos por los Indios y robos verificados en diversos puntos del Estado de Sonora. Conferencias de los Generales Topete y Carbó, con el General Crook, sopre la campana contra los salvajes, etc.; 15778, Topete to Minister of War and Marine, May 1, 1883; 16671, Topete to Minister of War and Marine, May 12, 1883.

[22] Bourke, Diary, LXVII, 32.

Dear Gen'l.

We ran on the Indians deserted camp yesterday morning on
top of the divide. They had camped there for several days; from
there their trails ran in several directions. . . . My plan now is to
move out in the morning and keep one day in advance of you. . . .
Some of the trails are about (4) four days old.

Respectfully,
Crawford.

The next day there came another message:

May 15 1883.

Dear Gen'l:

Scouts out yesterday report fresh trail of Indians going West,
with horses and cattle. You had better camp at place packers
designate until you hear from me again. I thought it best not to
take mules with me.

Respt.
E. Crawford.

P.S. I don't think the Indians know we are in the country.

John Rope reported that after several days of scouting, the
Apaches were cooking food while some of them went ahead
and looked through the glasses to see what they would find.

In a little while the scouts who had the glasses came back. They
had seen the Chiricahua camp on top of a ridge across the valley
[to the west], on the side of the other mountain. On a level place
near the camp all the horses of the Chiricahuas were grazing.
There were lots of them. We all hurried back, and there we could
see the camp all right. There were quite a few Chiricahuas in it.
Sieber sent two scouts back to tell the other soldiers and scouts
who were way behind to hurry up and reach our camp that night.
Some of the scouts were afraid. It was only about a mile across
the valley from where we were to the Chiricahua camp. That
night we could not sleep but set and talk in whispers. . . .

Now [at daylight] we looked at the Chiricahua camp again. There was lots of smoke coming up from it. We started out toward the camp. Part of the soldiers and scouts went on the left side and part on the right. In the middle went Alchise and his scouts. This way we were going to surround the Chiricahua camp before they found out we were here. One of the scouts on our side of the line saw two Chiricahua men riding toward the scouts. He told the others, and they waited to surround the two Chiricahuas. One sergeant had his gun all cocked ready to fire. The gun went off by accident, but even so the Chiricahuas did not seem to hear and kept right on coming. Then we scouts started shooting at them but missed. The two men jumped off their mules and ran off in the rocks and brush.

The premature shooting had sprung the trap. A general attack was made on the camp, during which some captives, women and children, were taken, Rope picking up three prisoners himself.

"This camp was Chihuahua's," wrote Rope, "and he and his brother had just come from the warpath with lots of cattle. The Chiricahuas had been butchering, and there was meat lying all around on the bushes to dry." While some of the scouts looted the camp, others rounded up the horse herd.

Two Chiricahua men got up on a high, rocky shoulder above us. They shot down at us a couple of times; then they yelled: "All right, you're doing this way with us now, but some time we will do the same way with you," and then they went off. . . . Only four [nine] of the Chiricahuas had been killed. One of these was an old woman; it was some San Carlos scouts who shot her. She had stood up when they came to her and asked them not to kill her but to take her captive instead.[23] We White Mountain men talked to the San Carlos scouts who shot her

[23] This was probably Chihuahua's aunt, whose slaying he bitterly resented, see below.

and said, "Why did you kill that old woman? You ought not to have killed her." The San Carlos men said they had come after these Chiricahuas and they were going to kill them.[24]

Meanwhile a courier had reached Crook with another message:

Gen'l:

The scouts ran across the Indians this A.M. in a cañon (2) two shots were fired at 2 Bucks and squaw by scouts which alarmed them and the whole camp is on the move. We will push after them as rapidly as possible. I think you had better come after us as rapidly as possible. Send whatever men can be spared. The scouts became very much excited. The bearer will bring you after us.

Resp't,
Crawford

Hastening ahead the command heard shots. "At 2 P.M. reports of distant musketry sounded in our ears," wrote Bourke. "Crawford and his scouts were fighting the Chiricahuas! There could be no mistake."[25]

Upon receiving the message, wrote the diarist, "the command pushed rapidly on, not making camp until after nightfall," but still short of the village. Captain Chaffee and his 6th Cavalry troop hurried on to the support of Crawford and his scouts, Bourke recorded. Desultory firing continued at long intervals during the afternoon, "just enough to attract attention and to convince listeners that our Indian scouts were still hanging on to the trail of the fleeing hostiles."

Crawford returned with the scouts late in the afternoon. They had "jumped" Bonito's rancheria at 2 o'clock killing (7) seven

24 Rope, "Experiences of an Indian Scout," *Arizona Historical Review*, Vol. VII, No. 2 (April, 1936), 59–62. His account is abbreviated here.

25 Bourke, Diary, LXVII, 49–50. All the above Crawford messages were copied by Bourke in his diary.

and capturing (5) five—(2) two boys, (2) little girls and one young woman, the daughter of Bonito. . . . They destroyed the rancheria, burning up the wicky-ups (between 20 and 30) and loading down 47 animals—mules and ponies—with plunder. This included the traditional riffraff of an Indian village— saddles, bridles, meat, mescal, blankets and clothing, and an occasional piece of more valuable booty obtained in their countless raids upon Mexicans & Americans. . . .

The procession coming down the mountain was unique and at times, laughable. The captured animals were weighted down with all manner of stuff, and the scouts themselves puffed and struggled under burdens, most of which had been carried home for glory only and would be thrown aside upon the first opportunity. . . .

The fight was made by our Apache scouts alone no white troops being present; altho' the result might have been better, yet it might also have been worse. Our scouts were too eager to engage; a serious fault, it is true, but a virtue compared with a disinclination to do the same thing. Not a casualty happened to a man on our side. This is the first time that the Chiricahuas have suffered so great a loss, without inflicting any punishment whatever upon their assailants. The attack has been made in the innermost recesses of what they have so long regarded as an impregnable stronghold—a fact, of itself, sufficient to disconcert them greatly. . . . All night long the mountain—the scene of the action—blazed with fire from the burning rancheria.[26]

Many of the Chiricahua warriors at this time were engaged in an extensive raid into Chihuahua under the leadership of Geronimo and thus were absent from their Sierra Madre retreat. At the time of the attack on the rancheria, they were returning, but still were several days distant. Yet what had happened, according to good authority, became known to

[26] Bourke, Diary, LXVII, 50–54.

them as a result of an intriguing quality, or purported talent, of their leader.

Betzinez, who was with the raiders, said that the band was eating one day on their return. "Geronimo was sitting next to me with a knife in one hand and a chunk of beef which I had cooked for him in the other. All at once he dropped the knife, saying, 'Men, our people whom we left at our base camp are now in the hands of U.S. troops!' "

This, Betzinez added, "was a startling example of Geronimo's mysterious ability to tell what was happening at a distance. I cannot explain it to this day. But I was there and saw it. No, he didn't get the word by some messenger. And no smoke signals had been made."[27]

When Betzinez recorded this, it might be pointed out, he was no mystic nor even dominated by Indian superstitions, traditional or otherwise. He was an old man, a Christian of many years standing, married to a white Christian missionary, and had rid himself, as he proudly said, of the superstitions of his pagan youth.

Lest one suspect that this was an isolated incident, one might cite the meticulous ethnologist, Morris E. Opler, who, in a discussion of shamanism in his thorough *An Apache Life-Way*, quotes an informant:

The shaman whose work has to do with war had a strong part in politics and could rise to a position of power. . . . Geronimo got political power from the religious side. He foresaw the results of the fighting, and they used him so much in the campaigns that he came to be depended upon. He went through his ceremony, and he would say, "You should go here; you should not go there." That is how he became a leader.[28]

[27] Betzinez, *I Fought With Geronimo*, 113.
[28] Opler, *An Apache Life-Way*, 200.

XIII   PERILS UNIMAGINED

General Crook now faced the most critical moments of his Mexico adventure. He had traveled to the heart of the gloomy and mysterious Mother Range, had located one camp of the hostiles only through the assistance of his captured guide, had fought—and scattered—this band, and thus had warned the hostiles throughout the mountains of his presence. He knew that they might now scatter like quail and that further pursuit would then be unfruitful if not impossible.

The loyalty of his scouts had been demonstrated to his own satisfaction, but even they could not perform a miracle, which would be necessary if he were to bring about another fight, perhaps a decisive one, between his forces and the recalcitrant warriors. In any event, Apaches did not fight "decisive" battles; it was not their nature. If there was a "decisive" action in Mexico, it must be that which already had taken place.

With no further power, and no means of forcing the hostiles to come in, Crook now had to depend upon persuasion, diplomacy, and, to some degree, upon sheer bluff if his mission was to succeed completely. The first requirement was to establish contact with the leaders. His action had to be as inclusive as possible, for, as he had often stated, if even a handful of hostiles remained out they could prove as unsettling and disturbing as though the whole Chiricahua people were loose.

Not only was Crook now forced to proceed by talks, instead of by arms, among the hostiles, he had to convince the white Americans and white Mexicans that he had fulfilled his mission, for the whites were at least as responsible for initiating and maintaining Indian hostilities as were the red men.

"After surprising and destroying Chatto's camp,[1] the situation presented certain very serious complications," wrote Crook in his *Annual Report*.

> The Indians were so thoroughly alarmed that to attempt further pursuit would be fruitless. We could never hope to catch them in the rugged peaks, and the effort would surely cost the lives of many men, each rock being a fortress from behind which the Chiricahuas would fight to the death with their breech-loading guns. The alternatives seemed presented: we must either return, let the excitement quiet down, and then, if permitted, steal back again and take the chances of another surprise, during which period the Chiricahuas would be continuing their depredations in Mexico and our own country; or, we must accept their surrender.

What he did not enlarge upon were the manifold difficulties in the way of bringing about their surrender, not least of which was how to contact the hostiles still out.

Fortunately captives had been taken, among them a young woman, the daughter of Bonito. It was she who was to prove the key to the success of the expedition at this point, for it

[1] Precisely whose camp the rancheria was is not clear. Sometimes it is called Bonito's, sometimes Chatto's, and sometimes even Chihuahua's. There were two rancherias together, according to some accounts. If this is true, they probably belonged to Chatto and Bonito separately. See notation on Crook map.

was through her that Crook was to establish contact with the important leaders. Another captive was the child of Nachez, son of Cochise. "The captives appeared to be much frightened, but behaved with great self-possession, considering their tender years," said Bourke.[2]

Crook carefully began his delicate work the next day.

He "had a talk with the oldest of the Chiricahua captives," the daughter of Bonito.

> He gave the girl provisions to last her back to her people and sent her with the older of the two little boys to open negociations [sic]. . . . The girl asserted that the Chiricahuas were anxious to make peace and had talked of dispatching (2) two messengers to the San Carlos to ask for terms. General Crook replied that he would move camp to-morrow to a point on the Bavispe a short distance (4 miles) from here and would there await for three (3) days any communication the enemy might wish to make.[3]

The scouts, flush with all their loot, resumed their gambling, meanwhile, to which they were passionately addicted. "Rumors," said Bourke, "have been flying around crediting our Apaches with having fallen upon inconceivable spoil. . . . All that can be said with certainty is that our savage allies are now 'flush' and are bucking the tiger with the air of Wall St. brokers; several of them are arrayed in Mexico sombreros of the loudest patterns, embroidered in gold and silver and entwined by a silver rattlesnake."[4]

Camp was moved next morning to a point five airline miles east-northeast of the burned-out rancheria, in a valley near the junction of two live streams. The site was surrounded by hills on which pickets were posted. A smoke signal was loosed

[2] Bourke, Diary, May 15 entry, LXVII, 52–53.

[3] *Ibid.*, 56–57.

[4] *Ibid.*, 59–60.

San Bernardino Ranch, located on the Mexican border, is one of the famous old establishments of early-day Arizona. From here Crook launched his Sierra Madre expedition in 1883. The ranch layout has not changed since his day.

The junction of the San Bernardino River (flowing from lower left to center) and the Bavispe River (flowing from middle left to right). Crook and his men turned up the Bavispe and traveled toward the mountains.

On the plaza at Bacerac, in a store like this one, or perhaps in this very store, the packers and scouts, with Al Sieber and Frank Monach the instigators, held their riotous dance on the Saturday night Crook's expedition arrived in 1883.

Huachinera sits at the foot of the Sierra Madre, and the Bavispe River flows from above. The stream on this side of the town is a branch of the Bavispe and is shown on the Crook map. The expedition traveled up this stream to Tesorababi, then turned southwest into the mountains.

This high ridge of the Sierra Madre rises south from Huachinera. According to the Crook map, the second García fight with the Apaches (April 25, 1883) took place on the reverse slope at the right end of this ridge, behind its highest point. Crook went into the mountains to the right of this ridge.

The interior of the Sierra Madre, showing the extreme roughness of the terrain.

This may be the ridge on which Chatto's and Bonito's ranch-
erías were located and where Crook fought in the action
which marked the climax of the Sierra Madre expedition.
Across the ridge is the valley of Nacori. It is difficult to pick
out the precise sites from the air, even on the basis of such
highly detailed maps as that of the Crook expedition, but this
appears to be the only ridge fitting its description—and that
of John Rope—as the locale of the fight. The photograph was
taken from the east looking west.

Upper Bavispe River, with the Sierra Madre. Crook camped
along this stream while he waited for the Apaches to come in
to talk and promise surrender.

to let the hostiles know where the base now was located, and precisely at noon answering signals curled upward from the mountains about. Forty-five minutes later Severiano[5] informed Crook that two squaws were approaching. "They were the sisters of Tu-klas (or Tu-lane)—one of our scouts— himself a Chiricahua, the only one of that band who had not broken out from the San Carlos," confided Bourke. Tu-lane had told the captive boy to tell his sister to come in and talk with him, and in response to that invitation, she had arrived. He now told her, "We have been all over looking for you people, not to kill you, but to bring you back to San Carlos to be friends. Tell this to Chihuahua."[6]

Then at three o'clock a picket's shout signaled the arrival of two more women, one afoot and the other mounted on a pony, furiously waving a white flag. Four others seated themselves above the camp, watching "the strange scene of animation far beneath." One of the two women who came in was a sister of Chihuahua,[7] one of the principal hostiles and the one Crook most wished to contact. She said the expedition had seized a white horse, with a Mexican saddle on which were black saddlebags, plus a bridle with silver bit. If they wanted

[5] Severiano is frequently mentioned in contemporary accounts of those days. He apparently was trusted and dependable. However, not much is known about him, not even his first name, if any. He was said by Gatewood to have been a Mexican, born in Sonora, captured as a youth by the Apaches, and married to a White Mountain squaw. Gatewood called him "excitable, nervous, with a lively imagination, rather poetic temperament and consequently considerable oratorical ability." His name may have been either Spanish or Apache. The Register of Enlistment of Scouts indicates he was dark, five feet, seven inches tall, and that he enlisted as a scout August 23, 1871, at the age of about thirty. He was a reliable interpreter, trusted alike by Indians and whites. Arizona Pioneers' Historical Society records.

[6] Rope, "Experiences of an Indian Scout," *Arizona Historical Review*, Vol. VII, No. 2 (April, 1936) 64.

[7] Rope says a sister of Geronimo, *ibid*., 64.

151

to talk with Chihuahua, they must first give this back. It was located and given her. She took it into the mountains.[8] Before leaving she told the general that her brother would come in "early to-morrow morning with his whole band and surrender." Then she hastily withdrew.

The woman was partially correct. The next day four women, a man, and a boy came into camp at 8:30 A.M., and within an hour sixteen men, women, and young children arrived. Then came Chihuahua himself, a mighty warrior and a great raider, determined to let no one forget his prominence. John Rope graphically describes his arrival:

> We could see someone riding that white horse over some rocky places at the foot of the mountain. It was Chihuahua, and he rode fast to our camp. On the end of his horse's tail was tied a strip of red cloth, and another strip of red cloth hung from under the bridle. In his belt he wore two pistols, and in his hand he carried a lance with a strip of red cloth tied around its end. He rode toward some of us scouts who were sitting under some oak trees. We all jumped up, not knowing what he intended to do. He asked where the head officer was, and we told him. Then he ran his horse right through us to General Crook's tent. He rode through soldiers and scouts alike, and they had to get out of his way. Mickey Free and Si-bi-ya-na (Severiano), who were the interpreters, followed him to the general's place. Chihuahua got off his horse in front of the tent, and there he shook hands with General Crook. He said, "If you want me for a friend, why did you kill that old woman, my aunt. If I was trying to make friends with someone, I would not go and raid their camp and shoot their relatives. It seems to me that you are lying when you speak about being friends."[9]

[8] *Ibid.*, 64.

[9] *Ibid.* Rope's description of this and subsequent events is on 64–67.

In this exchange one sees that the bold and vigorous hostile leader, who did not fear to ride alone, though fully armed, into an enemy camp, and who came not as a supplicant but as a complete equal to his counterpart, had some questions of his own to ask, although the statement about the slaying of his aunt and the attack on the village might have been to gain some initial advantage for himself and to put the talk initially on an equal footing. At any rate, having made his points, he accepted tobacco as a sign of friendship, or at least of openness, and some food "to take back with him," said Rope.

Bourke, describing Chihuahua as "a man upon whose lineaments great decision of character was imprinted," said that the two had "a very satisfactory talk." Afterwards Chihuahua "was given permission to go out and hunt up the remnant of his band, promising to have them all back by to-morrow,"[10] which was, to say the least, putting the most favorable cast to the conversations. Rope said that, having accepted tobacco and food, Chihuahua "got on his horse and rode off fast, right through us, the way he had come." Later Tu-lane's sister said that "Chihuahua felt bad about the way things had happened. He had said, 'It's no good, all these scouts and soldiers here,' and he told the women to get ready to move farther away, maybe south to the Aros River," whose nearest point was fifty airline miles distant. Obviously there was a difference of understanding about the success of this initial talk. However, Chihuahua did not move his camp far, after all, nor were the contacts to be terminated unsuccessfully.

On May 19 the American camp was moved about four and one-half miles northeast, "in pursuance of directions given by Chihuahua," said Bourke.[11]

[10] Bourke, Diary, LXVII, 65–66.
[11] Ibid., 69.

By noon of that day the number of Indians in camp, mostly women, children, and the aged, was one hundred. An informant said that "Loco had gone on to the San Carlos Reservation with 20 families, there to give himself up," but this report merely illustrates the vast difficulties involved in translating incidents, statements, and ideas back and forth, from one tongue to another. Loco had not gone north, nor had twenty of his families. But twenty members of Loco's family had gone before Crook arrived in the Sierra Madre and, while the general was south, would surrender at the reservation, although Loco himself had yet to come in. Translation difficulties caused no end of complexities. For example, Mickey Free was the primary translator from Apache to Spanish, but he knew nothing but "present-tense Spanish," and Severiano, who was entrusted with translating Mickey's Spanish to English, sometimes had difficulty even comprehending what Free meant to convey. This was a major hazard in dealing with the wild Chiricahuas, and, of course, translation of Crook's remarks and attitude into their language no doubt posed similar problems.

Geronimo and his thirty-six raiders in the state of Chihauhua, were soon to return. Tu-lane's sister "said she thought there was going to be more trouble" when the warriors returned, "and they found out what had happened, they would fight us," reported Rope. "She said we had better all look out." The Chiricahua women tore up flour sacks and posted white flags all around the camp "to let the Chiricahuas know we didn't want to fight." Warned that the warriors "might start shooting," Rope and the other scouts fashioned rude barricades for defense. During the night the women called up into the apparently empty hills, explaining who the invaders were and that they wanted to talk, not fight. "The

Chiricahua men up on the ridges heard them all right," Rope believed.

"After sunrise, when we had eaten we heard some Chiricahuas calling to us from the mountain. We could see lots of men up there together." Some scouts, acquainted with various of the hostiles, went out to talk with them, including a brother-in-law of Chatto. The scouts returned, and "then Tu-lane's brother gave a yell and ran into our camp. When we got there he threw his gun and belt on the ground. Then he said to Tu-lane, 'My brother, you have been looking for me, and now I am with you again. . . .' Then the two embraced each other. This was the first man to come in. Soon all the rest of the Chiricahua men came in, except the chiefs, who stayed apart."[12]

Bourke wrote, "From our Apache scouts I [learned] that this was a big raiding party which had been raising Hell in Chihuahua. . . . Those who didn't dare to come down [that is, the chiefs and war leaders] perched on the battlements of the high rocky bluff overhanging camp, where they looked like so many hawks, or vultures, perhaps greedy for blood. . . . They sent word that they wanted to talk with General Crook." Bourke wrote that the general replied that if they wished to see him they could come in without fear of molestation, but Rope's account varies sharply. It is Rope's version which was distorted and, later on in the United States, caused vast doubts about whether Crook "captured" Geronimo, or the Indian captured the general. The major question remains, which version is true?

"General Crook was off by himself hunting birds with a shotgun," reported John Rope. "When he was there, all the

[12] Rope, "Experiences of an Indian Scout," *Arizona Historical Review*, Vol. VII, No. 2 (April, 1936) 66–67.

Chiricahua chiefs came to him. They grabbed his gun away and took the birds he had shot. They said he had been shooting toward them. Mickey Free and Si-bi-ya-na went there. They all sat on the ground and talked. After about two hours the general came back with all the Chiricahua chiefs to camp."[13] Bourke wrote simply that "while we were eating supper, Hieronymo was ushered in to have a talk with General Crook. His men entered in the usual Apache style, (2) two by this trail and (2) two by that; the fear of treachery and ambuscade ever-present to their minds."[14]

The Rope version, embellished and touched up by lively imaginations, was printed by the *Chicago Times*, some time in October, 1883, before the bulk of the Chiricahua warriors had come in to the reservation. A clipping, not precisely dated, is pasted in Bourke's Diary.[15] It attributes the account to a "Mr. Rochester Ford, of St. Louis, returned recently to his home from his summer vacation . . . in southern Arizona," a man who said he got the story from "personal knowledge" and interviews with unnamed officials. According to Ford's story:

> Gen. Crook, led by his White Mountain Apache scouts, was one evening toward dusk betrayed into a narrow canyon and there camped. During the night all the White Mountain Apache scouts left the camp and took up their positions on the hillsides with the Chiricahuas who had surrounded Crook and had determined upon the massacre of his entire force at daylight next morning.

However, a squaw reassured them as to Crook's intentions, asserting he had come

13 *Ibid.*, 67.
14 Bourke, Diary, LXVII, 76.
15 Bourke, Diary, LXXII, 99, 102.

to guarantee them immunity from harm and to take them back to the reservation where they would be kept at the expense of the government without having to do any work. . . .

A council was held, and they decided to postpone the massacre until noon the next day. . . . In the morning Crook awoke [and] from behind every rock on both sides of the canyons he saw pointed down toward his camp the rifles of the Chiricahuas. Turning to Capt. Crawford . . . he said: "We are surrounded and possibly shall all be massacred, and we might as well go to our fate bravely. Give me my shot-gun. I will go up on the side of the hill and pretend not to see them."

Taking his gun, about 7 o'clock in the morning, he went up on the side of the hill, but was no sooner out of sight of his camp than he was, of course, taken prisoner by the Chiricahuas. This enabled him to have a talk with them. An interpreter was sent for, and Crook was kept there till almost noon. He had to accede to the demands of the Chiricahuas in order to escape with his own life and to save the lives of his men. . . . [The Chiricahuas] never promised to come in, and when Crook made the proposition to them that they should, they laughed at him. . . .

It would seem likely that something of what Rope reported was true. If this is the case, one can only admire the intrepidity of Crook. Hearing that the chiefs wanted him to come up and talk with them, realizing that he could not appear ready to be ordered about by his enemies, yet aware of the vital significance of such a conference and the most delicate state of the present affairs, he literally took his life in his hands and pretended to go bird-shooting alone, directly into the jaws of the volatile enemy. He allowed himself to be "taken" by the hard-bitten Apaches—all in order to open direct negotiations. Although fond of shooting, the officer would scarcely have selected this particular moment to go about the sport, unless he had a purpose in mind; the purpose

157

was as daring as any recorded in the annals of Indian war. Nothing but respect can be returned to Crook for taking the perilous gamble.

If this analysis is correct, the question remains, what did Crook say to the warrior chiefs, and how did he persuade them to come into his camp? Throughout his life Crook insisted that one must never lie to an Indian, and he no doubt regarded whatever he promised them on that hillside as binding. We can never know, because no participant ever told what was said there, but Crook must have granted them some assurances which were plausible enough to convince them to accompany him into what they considered the enemy's camp. Thus, it would seem probable that their ultimate "surrender" was not truly unconditional, but on the basis of some sort of understanding, the preliminaries of which were worked out on this sunny morning.

This in no way belittles Crook's remarkable achievement, but rather enhances one's respect for it. The general had two major parties to please—the hostiles, in order to persuade them to come in, and the American settlers, so as to get them to accept his feat and allow the Indians to come home safely. This was not an easy compromise to arrange, but George Crook did it.

Bourke reported that on this day, May 20, nearly forty principal Chiricahuas filtered into camp, "a piratical gang, surely, one that would have made the fortune of any manager who should place them on the stage as the 'Pirates of Penzance.' There wasn't a weak face in the line; not a soft feature. Each countenance was indicative of boldness, cunning and cruelty." A brief meeting was followed, later in the evening, by another, longer one.[16]

16 Bourke, Diary, LXVII, 77.

He vividly describes Geronimo's several interviews with Crook. Bourke wrote that at first Crook "declined to have anything to do with him" beyond pointing out that the advantage now lay on the American side. "This reply disconcerted 'Geronimo'; he waited for an hour, to resume the conversation, but received no encouragement." A second time he begged for peace, and Crook told him he "could make up his mind as to what he wanted, peace or war." Geronimo the next day, according to Bourke, said it was peace he wanted. Repeatedly, in subsequent interviews, he insisted he wanted to surrender.[17]

In all of this Bourke no doubt reflects accurately the general trend of the negotiations, but on Crook's side much of it was bluff, designed to disarm and win over the enemy, and in this it was successful. Had Geronimo actually opted for war, all would have been lost, and Crook knew it. He bid high on a hole card that was a blank, but he put it over.

The next morning four of the hostile leaders joined Bourke and Fiebeger for breakfast: Geronimo, Tcha-nol-haye, a brother of "Navajo Bill" (his presence as a Chiricahua leader no doubt was the reason Bill had been sent on the scout into Mexico earlier), Chatto, and Nachez. "They all seemed to be in pleasant humor and consumed with relish the bread, beans and coffee set before them; pork they would not touch," observed the captain.[18] Several other warriors rode into camp during the afternoon, including the important Ka-ya-ten-nae, or "Looking Glass," as his name usually is translated, although there are other versions of what the Apache word meant. Although a young man, he had succeeded Victorio as war chief of the Warm Springs Indians, and took

---

[17] Bourke, *An Apache Campaign in the Sierra Madre*, 101–102.
[18] Bourke, Diary, LXVII, 78.

over his band of seventy-nine, including fifty-three fighting men. Ka-ya-ten-nae was said never to have been on a reservation, although Betzinez reported that he had accompanied the raiders who forced the Loco *émeute* from San Carlos, and he was willing now to listen to talk about that place.

The day following, five pitiful figures, Mexican women, one of whom carried a child, labored into camp from the spot where they had been abandoned by the raiding party. They reported that they had been captured not far from Casas Grandes, the Chiricahuas intending to hold them as hostages for return of women and children taken in the García fight, but they were left to their own devices when the presence of Crook and his command excited the immediate attention of the warriors. The expedition personnel gently cared for them, clothed and fed them, and eventually they were turned over to the Mexican consul at Tucson for repatriation.

Among the Chiricahua leaders was one named Dji-li-kine, called by Rope "a chief because he was about the best fighter of any of them [although] a little man and not as tall as an old-fashioned musket." Even so, Rope added, the other Chiricahua chiefs "were like nothing to him, and they actually did what he advised." He was Geronimo's father-in-law, but, unlike his son-in-law, he was not blindly belligerent. He was a man of good sense, one who listened to what Crook had to say. Thus he refused to take part in the brewing treachery that posed the next major threat to the success of the general's expedition.

After a council, the Chiricahua chiefs, on about May 22 or 23, "said that this night they were going to have a dance for all the scouts and let the Chiricahua girls dance with them."

By Apache custom, in dances of this sort, the male had to

160

pay something to the girl with whom he danced, but this time, promised the chiefs, all would be free—as part of the trap they planned to set. Then "the Chiricahua men planned to kill the scouts. It didn't matter if they themselves got killed," reported Rope.

The chiefs called Dji-li-kine to their council and told him of their plans, seeking his approval because of his great fighting reputation and the respect in which they all held him. But Dji-li-kine abruptly refused "because the White Mountain people are relatives of mine" and stalked off. The council sent for him once more, and Geronimo assured him, "we mean to do as we told you." Dji-li-kine angrily retorted: "I told you already that I would not help you do this." He strode away, then returned and said bitterly, "You chiefs don't mean anything to me. I have been with you many times and helped you kill lots of Mexicans and whites, and that's the way you got the clothes you are wearing now. I am the one who has killed these people for you, and you have just followed behind me. I don't want to hear you talking this way with me again!"

The Chiricahuas stubbornly went ahead with their plans and that evening started their dance anyway. But their carefully laid plot was not to be carried out.

It did not succeed because of one potent reason: Al Sieber. On previous occasions he had proved a key man at trying times; he had won the respect and unqualified trust of countless army officers and others engaged against the Apaches, and now he nipped this gravest threat to success of the Crook expedition.

Sieber had learned of the dance and what it meant. He was also aware of the death that day of one of the scouts, Dja-nde-zi, who had made a perilous incursion into Mexico in search of the hostiles because he was well thought of by the Chiricahuas. "Sieber sent word for them to stop the dance on account of this, so they did."[19] Had it not been for this apparently simple action, the dance might have continued, the mercurial Chiricahuas might have been moved psychologically to spring their trap, and disaster could have resulted. Sieber's knowledge of the Apaches, his understanding of their ways and their rigid adherence to ritual, their manner of thought, and his quick action and resourcefulness, saved the day. Yet he was never given particular credit for this, by Bourke or anyone else. It is possible that the other whites were not entirely aware of how closely they had escaped, although Rope and presumably some other scouts well knew of it, or heard about it later on. It is not unlikely that the full story was unrevealed until Rope dictated his memoirs, and there it has lain ever since.

Wednesday, May 23, old Nana came in, the incredible warrior of ancient vintage who had often been reported killed and would be so reported at various times in the future. "This old chief has a very strong face—one showing that he is powerful for good or evil," noted Bourke. "He is still prominent and influential among the Chiricahuas, altho' the principal chief seems now to be Kau-tinne [Ka-ya-ten-nae]. . . . Fifteen (15) Indians all told formed the band of Nane's."[20]

Geronimo and other leaders had left the camp, presumably to hunt up their people and also, no doubt, to scour the countryside for loose stock. Crook moved camp a short distance, and on May 25 at about dusk, Loco and his band came

[19] Rope, "Experiences of an Indian Scout," *Arizona Historical Review*, Vol. VII, No. 2 (April, 1936), 68–69.
[20] Bourke, Diary, LXVIII, 5–6.

in. Chatto and his family came in later that night. Loco, said Bourke, "has by all odds the best face of all the Chiricahuas." Crook talked with them the next morning. Chatto reported that their families were "very much scattered" and that he had been unable to locate Juh or his tiny band. As a matter of fact, Juh and one or two others never did come in, and Juh himself was killed not long after in a fall near the Casas Grandes River.[21] The two leaders urged Crook to remain in camp four more days to give the hostiles time to come in, and the general, although seriously short of rations for the growing crowd, agreed reluctantly to do so, although Bourke, "more than ever dissatisfied" with the Chiricahuas, had little faith they would return. "Present appearances point to a plan to work off all surplus women and children and decrepit men upon this command, leaving the Apache incorrigibles free to continue depredations upon Mexico," he grumbled.[22]

While Crook was camped at this point, an excited Apache scout dashed into camp one day and reported that "he had seen Mexican soldiers who would have nothing to do with him. When he tried to communicate, they fired upon him. . . ." Lieutenant Forsyth, Al Sieber, and ten cavalrymen hurriedly mounted and were sent out to contact the Mexicans. After a fifteen-mile ride they returned reporting no luck. The next day, however, Sieber took a few of Chaffee's troopers and searched again "and confirmed the truth of the story." He found where the Mexicans had rounded up what loose animals they encountered and had driven them from the mountains.[23]

Late that day, May 28, the chiefs returned, Geronimo,

[21] Thrapp, *Conquest of Apacheria*, 291n.
[22] Bourke, Diary, LXVIII, 20–21.
[23] *Ibid.*, 24–25.

Chatto, Kay-ya-ten-nae, Chihuahua, Bonito, and the others, except, of course, for Juh. They conferred with the commander, and the next morning, Tuesday, "from an early hour General Crook was in consultation with the Chiricahua chiefs and head men." Geronimo and Bonito took breakfast with the officers and packers on the thirtieth, and then they went south. The command with its horde of Indians swung out north on the long journey home. With them went 273 women and children and 52 warriors, including Loco, Nana, and Bonito.

The fact that the major leaders, except for the two aged ones and Bonito, did not return with his command left Crook in an unenviable position. He knew that eventually they would come in, but he had no idea when; time, supremely significant to white Americans, meant less than nothing to an Apache.

"Some of the Chiricahuas," commented Rope, "asked for permission to gather a lot of horses from the Mexicans before they left Mexico. General Crook gave them permission." He could do nothing else. "Lots of the Chiricahuas and their chiefs went, but General Crook didn't try to stop them. They did not like the little San Carlos ponies and wanted to get some good horses before going back. Dji-li-kine went with them also."[24]

Crook reported, in his summary, that the chiefs had said they wanted to make peace and return to San Carlos.[25]

I replied that they had been committing atrocities and depredations upon our people and the Mexicans, and that we had become tired of such a condition of affairs and intended to wipe

[24] Rope, "Experiences of an Indian Scout," *Arizona Historical Review*, Vol. VII, No. 2 (April, 1936), 69.
[25] What follows is from his *Annual Report*, 1883.

them out; that I had not taken all this trouble for the purpose of making them prisoners; that they had been bad Indians, and that I was unwilling to return without punishing them as they deserved; that if they wanted a fight, they could have one any time they pleased. I told them that the Mexican troops were moving in from both sides, and it was only a matter of days until the last of them should be under the ground.

The best thing for them to do was to fight their way out if they thought they could do it. I kept them waiting for several days, and each day they became more and more importunate. Jeronimo and all the chiefs at last fairly begged me to be taken back to San Carlos. . . . [They said]: "We give ourselves up, do with us as you please."

Crook noted that his rations were running dangerously low, and he could not remain in the Sierra Madre while the chiefs gathered up their people. He would have to start back by easy stages, trusting them to catch up. In his initial report of his journey, Crook stated that "by the terms of the treaty, my operations were limited to the time of the fight," and added: the chiefs "assured me every one of the band should come in if I would remain a short time; but the terms of the treaty embarrassed me greatly, and being in that rough region, with rations rapidly disappearing, there being between three and four hundred Chiricahuas to feed, I was compelled to return with the Chiricahuas."[26]

It will be noted that Crook made no mention of the treaty difficulties in his *Annual Report*, and in point of fact it was not a very good argument. That of dwindling rations was better, and entirely valid, but the real situation was that Crook had no means, except psychological pressure, to force

[26] Crook to AAG, Military Division of the Pacific, June 12, 1883, from Silver Creek, Arizona Territory. Printed textually in the *New York Herald*, June 13, 1883.

the Apaches to return to the United States with him or to do anything they did not wish to do.

However, he saw clearly one compelling lure that would bring them back, and this he promptly seized. By bringing in most of their women and children, and placing them on the reservation, he could rest assured that ultimately the warriors would all return, for family ties are very strong among the Apache people. Thus, facing a real quandary, the bearded officer carefully engineered conditions to bring about the results he desired, and he was, at long last, to be fully vindicated.

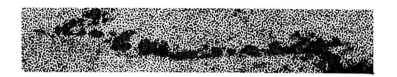

XIV IT IS FINISHED

Of the journey home, not much remains to report. The command left their Sierra Madre redoubt on May 30 and straggled along for fifteen miles over an eight thousand-foot divide before descending to camp at the point where a "broad, perfectly distinct trail" led off to the east, for Casas Grandes. Here was found, carved on the red inner bark of a mountain laurel, the message: "El 11 Battn Pasó Aquí 21° de Mayo '83," (The 11th Battalion passed here, 21st of May, '83),[1] evidence to support Crook's warning to the Apaches that Mexican forces were co-operating with his. No doubt this notice was left to advise the American column, if it came that way, of the penetration thus far into the Sierra Madre of the Chihuahua forces of General Raguero. There had been, of course, other evidences of co-operation, including the García fight with Apaches within the mountains before the American column arrived. The outskirts of the range were alive with military forces, but only Crook's had penetrated the massif deeply.

"Everyone is desirous to get home again," reported Bourke the next day, "so there's no delay in leaving camp. We were

[1] Bourke, Diary, LXVIII, 32; Crook, *Annual Report*, 1883, Appendix E.

on the march at 5.22 A.M. following by a trail, known only to the Chiricahuas, which led almost directly North, along the backbone of what must be the main ridge of the Sierra Madre. The pine forest was dense."[2]

On June 1, Geronimo caught up with the command for the last time, arriving after it had gone into camp. He arrived late, had a long talk with Crook, and left again at sunrise.[3]

The exodus continued. Crook led his people up through the wilderness, between the populated parts of Sonora on the west and those of Chihuahua on the east, hoping to avoid Mexicans, whether military forces, ranchers, or chance passersby, because if he met such, complications might ensue. Crook was lucky. On June 2 the group descended to the upper flow of the Río Janos, keeping along it for several leagues before camping, and the next day continuing to follow the stream. "We pushed along as fast as the condition of animals and of women and children would permit," noted Bourke.[4] They were camped on a bluff on the east side of the creek when a fresh catastrophe almost engulfed them.

> A careless Chiricahua squaw had set fire to the grass behind us and under the impetus of a high wind, the fierce flames were rushing down upon camp. There was not a moment to be lost; all hands were turned out—soldiers, scouts, squaws, Chiricahua warriors and children. Each bore a branch of willow or cotton-wood, a blanket or piece of canvas. The conflagration had already seized the hill-crest nearest our position and like a red-throated bull-dog kept quiet for a moment as if examining the victims upon which it was soon to spring. Brownish and grey clouds poured upward in compact masses, reaching to the zenith

[2] Bourke, Diary, LXVIII, 34.

[3] *Ibid.*, 37.

[4] *Ibid.*, 39.

and at their feet, a long line of scarlet flame flashed and leaped
high in air. . . . It was a grand, but terrible sight. . . . The heat
created a vacuum and the air pouring in made whirlwinds which
sent the black funnels of soot, winding and twisting with the
symmetry of hour-glasses, almost to where the sun was supposed to be.

"Here she comes!" yelled Forsyth. "Here she comes," echoed
Gatewood, "Here she comes"—shouted Zeiber, Bowman, West
and Chaffee. She *was* coming.

With a sullen roar, the wild beast the fire flung its tawny mane
of cloud high in air and flashed its bloody fangs of flame; and
then, before one could tell how or where or whence it came, fire
was on all sides. Our men stood up to their work and the swish!
swish! swish! of willow brooms let the flames know the camp
was not going to be surrendered without a struggle. We won the
day; that is, we saved our camp, our heads and a sufficiency of
pasturage. On every side was a zone of destruction over which
hung a dun mantle of stifling mist. . . . One of the Cavalry
horses,—a bit leg-weary, led by a trooper behind the column,
had its tail and fetlocks burned off.[5]

This campsite, although not marked on the map, through
someone's oversight, was probably near the gates through
which the river flows to the Casa de Janos, eighteen miles
airline southwest of Janos itself.

Well out of the mountains, the command and its convoyed
horde moved northwest all next day, around the curve of foothills, to camp on Aliso Creek "not far from the position where
the Mexican troops, under General [*sic*] Garcia, last year
ambuscaded the Apaches and wrought such havoc among
their women and children." Under a mistaken belief that
water could be found where Colonel Forsyth had camped at
that time, the command pushed on, "passing the battlefield

[5] *Ibid.*, 39–41.

with its suggestive [relics]—of bones, skulls, Indian baskets and dresses,—and graves of the Mexican officers and men who perished in the struggle." John Rope reported that "some of us scouts went over to see the battleground. There were many bleached-out bones, pieces of women's dresses, and lots of beads scattered on the ground. . . . We shouldn't have gone to look at this place, but we did it anyway." Western Apaches believe that to go near graves or places where others have been killed might bring sickness or evil upon the interlopers, but obviously this belief was not held universally.[6]

Finding no water, the command marched back past the battlefield to the foothills and camped near abundant springs. As the hunters brought in enough antelope, it was a pleasant camp.[7]

The march continued on subsequent days, once in a while being enlivened by further grass fires, but otherwise it was uneventful.

During the long weeks of his absence there were sporadic rumors, usually picked up by the press, that Crook and his party had run into disaster of one sort or another. On May 10 the *New-York Tribune* carried a dispatch from Chicago which said, "The officers of General Sheridan's headquarters in this city do not credit the rumors of a disaster to General Crook's column. While it is true there have been no recent advices from General Crook in person, they are in the way of receiving quick communications from any point . . . in case of an engagement, and particularly so in case of a disaster." On May 29 the *Tribune* reported to an increasingly anxious public that "no further information relative to Gen-

[6] Rope, "Experiences of an Indian Scout," *Arizona Historical Review*, Vol. VII, No. 2 (April, 1936), 70, 70n.

[7] Bourke, Diary, LXVIII, 45–46.

eral Crook's movements has been received at the War Department," but added that Adjutant General Richard C. Drum "is disposed to credit the report that General Crook has engaged the Apaches and defeated them." Why, in the absence of official reports, he chose to credit this rumor was not stated. No word from Crook himself was received from May 1, when his command plunged into Mexico, until June 11, after it had reached United States soil once more, although there had been Mexican reports from Bavispe and Bacerac of its progress through those communities on the way south.

The *New York Herald* had Randall with the command, but he was unable to file anything until the column returned. So this enterprising paper secured an unnamed "special correspondent" and sent him to Chihuahua, hoping he could interview officials there and learn something, and perhaps eventually reach Janos, the frontier town most likely to be a news fount. However, it told its readers on May 17 that "the Central Mexican Railroad officers say there are serious doubts of the correspondent reaching Janos. It cannot be disguised that the Mexican military chieftains are alarmed about Crook as he has, at least, undertaken the boldest venture of any American soldier."

On May 21 the special correspondent forwarded "interviews with leading officials" of Chihuahua about the Crook expedition.

"His entry into Mexico is considered of doubtful legality," said the correspondent, "but everybody is glad that he has made it."

He reviewed the Crook interviews with officials of Sonora and Chihuahua.

It was explained that no permission to make a campaign on

Mexican soil could be accorded him, as it would be against the treaty stipulations and international law. At the same time neither the Governor of Sonora nor of Chihuahua would interfere should he desire to follow up the hostiles. This arrangement, however, has not satisfied the authorities at the city of Mexico, and despatches have been sent to Sonora and Chihuahua asking an explanation. This fact has leaked out and caused great indignation among the best Mexican citizens. . . .

Don Juan Zubiran, Mayor of Chihuahua, for several years Consul of Mexico in the United States, says. . . . it is all very well for [officials] sitting at their ease in Washington and the city of Mexico to split straws over treaties, but those who live upon the borders of Sonora and Chihuahua, where nearly every family has lost a loved one, have other thoughts, and are determined that a few worthless savages must not be allowed to rob and murder any longer. The same feeling prevails in Arizona and New Mexico.

Don Juan Zubiran added: "I look upon Crook as a frontier savior. . . . We people of the frontier have closed our eyes on this treaty business, but diplomatic correspondence in regard to Crook's movements is going on between the two governments, and the longer Crook remains upon Mexican soil the more complicated the situation becomes, and many think, when the campaign is over, we will hear of courts martial on both sides of the line."[8]

Then on May 31, Arizona Department Assistant Adjutant General James P. Martin hurriedly relayed information to the Presidio at San Francisco that "Loco's wife, son, son-in-law, daughter, grandchildren and several others, altogether six bucks and 14 women and children gave themselves up" on the road to Fort Apache, and were being held as prisoners of war.[9] Britton Davis was asked by Martin to get further in-

[8] *New York Herald*, May 22, 1883.

formation out of them, and, above all, to discover what they knew of Crook's movements. On June 6, Davis replied.

"Sixty-six days ago Mexican troops surprised hostiles in south Sierra Madres," he reported, referring to García's fight in the mountains before Crook penetrated them. "These Indians were cut off from the main body and three days after fight started for reservation. One went back to bring Loco, but Loco is too old to travel and told them to come without him. . . . Indians knew nothing of General Crook when they left, but knew that the country was full of troops and if attacked will fight until whipped and then scatter through the Sierra Madres." The band reported that the hostiles had more than one hundred fighting men. The word from Loco's family was foreboding, and they were dubious about Crook's chances to contact and bring in any important segment of the Apaches, although they added that the "Indians are commanded by Geronimo and will not fight if they can help it."[10]

Still endeavoring to avoid any contact with Mexicans, Crook led his people through the wasteland northwesterly, threaded a narrow canyon in the southern reaches of the Peloncillo Mountains, passed between them and the Cocosperas, and reached the outbound trail a few miles south of San Bernardino Springs on June 9. They camped at that point. Here, in quiet celebration, "Gen. Crook called us all up to his tent and distributed the contents of the only bottle of liquor left in camp," the quart of "very good brandy" Samaniego had given him at Bacerac eons ago.[11] The next day, a bright Sunday morning, at about eleven o'clock, Gen-

<hr>

[9] LS613DA1883 Martin to AAG, Military Division of the Pacific, May 31, 1883.

[10] LS639DA1883 Martin to AG, Army, Washington, D.C., June 6, 1883.

[11] Bourke, Diary, LXVIII, 57.

eral Crook led the straggling party across the border and to Major Biddle's camp.

"Nice morning, Colonel," he is reported to have greeted Biddle, matter-of-factly.

"Straightway [he] struck out for a wash basin which he had spied, and was soon engaged in performing his ablutions, after which he threw himself upon a camp stool and engaged in conversation about his campaign in an offhand way, as if hunting the fiercest and most cruel foe on the continent, in the wildest and most inaccessible country to be found, was a matter of every-day occurrence."[12]

Crook's abrupt reappearance in Arizona, with hundreds of Apache prisoners and the promise that the rest of the important hostiles were coming in to surrender, brought him a flood of congratulatory messages, although Martin's telegram, "Great rejoicing among your friends the world over. Your campaign universally believed to be the grandest event in Indian hostilities in America,"[13] might have been a shade too enthusiastic. Nevertheless, it was an accomplishment of monumental proportions, even if a rapt summation by one biographer, that "Crook had performed the incredible feat of subduing the Chiricahuas eight months after he took control of the Department,"[14] is a bit more than the evidence supports. It would be another year before the last of the hostiles returned to San Carlos. Meanwhile they would continue their depredations in Mexico. There was no question, however, but that Crook's feat was a major one.

The *New-York Tribune* spoke for much of the nation's

[12] An article, probably originating with information from A. Frank Randall, June 13, 1883.

[13] LS672DA1883 Martin to Crook, Willcox, June 15, 1883.

[14] *General George Crook: His Autobiography* (ed. and annot. by Martin F. Schmitt), 248.

press when it editorially termed the expedition a "brilliant success" and doubted that the Mexican government would ever complain over any slight treaty-stretching that might have accompanied it.[15]

Yet as the weeks and months passed and the hostile chiefs failed to come in, as they had promised Crook and as he had promised the nation, the adulation turned to doubt and, in some quarters, to active hostility toward the general and his campaign. There even began to be heard reports that, far from having "captured" the Apaches, they, in effect, had captured him. The story told by Rope, of Crook's lone sortie into the hands of the warrior-leaders, was discovered, seized upon, embroidered, and used to illustrate this exaggerated thesis.[16]

The criticism was allayed to some extent when the hostiles at long last began to filter in. (Nonetheless, the hypothesis that Crook was "taken" by the Indians is still heard in uninformed circles in the Southwest.) Crook, although professing the utmost unconcern, had begun to feel uneasy. He sent Britton Davis to the border to await the Indians, or speed them up, if they were encountered. Davis sent scouts as deep into Mexico as they dared to go, but no contact was made. Yet, with the families of the hostiles securely in hand, Crook knew that the warriors ultimately would come in. And they did.

Thirteen Chiricahuas (eight warriors and five women and children) suddenly turned up.

In late October, Nachez and nine other Chiricahua warriors arrived.[17] Captain Rafferty, assigned to the border to

[15] *New-York Tribune*, June 14, 1883.

[16] For a discussion of this matter and of its origins, see Thrapp, *Conquest of Apacheria*, 295–302.

[17] Crawford to Crook, November 1, 1883, Hayes Collection.

await the hostiles, on November 16 brought to San Carlos 90 Chiricahuas, among them probably Ka-ya-ten-nae, Chihuahua, and Mangas, three of the most important men. Other small bands had made their way in. By the end of November there were 423 Chiricahuas, including 83 men, some of them war leaders, on the reservation.[18] Another small band arrived on December 20. Then, on February 7, 1884, Chatto and 19 others came in, and later that month Geronimo crossed the line with his people[19] and about 350 head of stolen livestock, which ultimately was taken from him and sold, the proceeds ($1,762.50) being turned over to Mexico for distribution to the original owners.[20] One last group, of a score or more, did not arrive at San Carlos until May 15, 1884. Crook conceded that "this party should have come in with Geronimo"[21] He added that "the Indians all agree that there are now [no] Indians of either of these bands [the Chiricahuas, or the Warm Springs] or from the White Mountain reservation, in Mexico, and I believe their statements are true. . . . I am convinced that they are all satisfied and perfectly contented and will give no further trouble if treated with common fairness."[22]

The task was finished, at last.

In a letter to Herbert Welsh, of the Indian Rights Association, Crook, in mid-summer, 1884, expressed his "firm

[18] Crook to AAG, Military Division of the Pacific, November 24, 1883, Hayes Collection.

[19] Davis lists some of these arrivals. See, *The Truth About Geronimo*, 69–101.

[20] Crook to AG, Army, Washington, D.C., August 16, 1884, Hayes Collection.

[21] Crook to AAG, Military Division of the Pacific, May 17, 1884, Hayes Collection.

[22] *Ibid.*

belief that there is not in your own state of Pennsylvania a village of same population more peaceable and law-abiding than the 5000 Apaches on the San Carlos Reservation,"[23] and he spoke the simple truth. From near-chaos in Southwestern Indian affairs, Crook had achieved in less than two years near-complete tranquility. It is perhaps not too much to say that there was not another officer in the Indian-fighting army of that day who could have wrought this remarkable change in a like space of time. Why could Crook do it? Hints, I believe, may be found in his letter to Welsh.

It is not to be denied that the Apache is the fiercest and most formidable of all our Indians, when upon the war-path. Opinion may differ as to the place in the scale of intelligence the Apache should occupy. . . . Speaking for myself, after a somewhat extended experience of over 32 years duration, with the various Indian tribes from British America to Mexico, from the Missouri River to the Pacific Ocean, I do not hesitate to put the Apache at the very head for natural intelligence and discernment. . . . Were he a Greek or a Roman, we should read with pride and enthusiasm of his determination to die rather than suffer wrong . . . [but] it is not always possible to do justice to his virtues or to consider his faults as identical with those of which we ourselves should be guilty under similar provocation.

He discussed how to convert the Apache from a warrior-nomad to an economically productive and peaceful individual, to transform him "from an Ishmaelite into a property owner." In the past, Crook believed, and from the pathetic story they related to him, "they had been systematically and outrageously plundered by a gang of sharks thinly disguised as Indian Agents and others."[24]

[23] Crook to Welsh, July 16, 1884, Hayes Collection.
[24] *Ibid.*

From all this, one can detect the principal precepts accounting for Crook's influence among, and lasting control over, the volatile Apaches: his respect for their capacities, his willingness to accept them on a fully equal footing with whites, together with his relentless determination—and capacity—to reward the good and punish the evildoers among them. There was no American, aside from the professional ethnologists, who better comprehended the Apache mind, and no American at all who as fully understood and appreciated their warlike spirit and how best to control it and divert it into useful channels.

Crook was no paragon. A human being, he had faults, as have all others. But he also possessed great virtues, many of which appear in his management of the wild Chiricahuas. Had it not been for unfortunate circumstances a year hence, they might well have remained at peace and in progress.

So large a force as Crook met up with in the Sierra Madre never again was out. When Geronimo and Chihuahua, a year later, broke out, they could take only a handful of warriors with them, and many of those who did go were dissatisfied and leaped at the first good opportunity to come in.

Surely the Crook expedition was the climactic event in the Apache wars.

Had his superiors understood Crook as well as he understood the Indians, he might have settled the later Geronimo uprising, prevented the permanent exile of the Chiricahuas from Arizona, and seen them securely on the road toward economic independence and tribal well-being. No other man could have done this, and none attempted it. That proved to be the ultimate tragedy for this great band of Apaches.

178

BIBLIOGRAPHY

MANUSCRIPT MATERIALS, UNPUBLISHED DOCUMENTS,
COLLECTIONS

Archivos de la Nacion de Mexico; "Convenios en tropas Americanas y Mexicanas respecto a la persecución de los Indios hóstiles. —Nombramiento del Jefe de las fuerzas Federales in el Estado de Sonora, en el General Bernardo Reyes.—Solicitan Destacamentos Federales en los Pueblos de Bacadihuache y Nacorí, por ataque de los Indios y otros diversos asuntos sobre los mismos bárbaros." 114814/11874 Secretario de Guerra y Marina, 1882. "Partes de novedades relativos a asesinatos cometidos por los Indios y robos verificados en diversos puntos del Estado de Sonora, Conferencias de los Generales Topete y Carbó, con el General Crook, sobre la campaña contra los salvajes.—Projecto del Coronel Mexicano en Arizona, sobre el establecimiento de Cantones Militares on la Frontera, para protejar los Estados de Chihuahua y Sonora." 11481-4/12221, Secretario de Guerra y Marina, 1883, Cuaderno 12.

Arizona Pioneers' Historical Society Archives, Tucson. Files of or pertaining to many Indian-war figures. George Crook, "The Apache Problem," typescript. Joseph F. Fish, "History of Arizona," unpublished manuscript. Carl T. Hayden Collection of documents on many Arizona pioneers. Gatewood Collection of documents pertaining to the career of Charles B. Gatewood.

Bancroft Library, Berkeley, California. Arizona manuscripts include brief biographical accounts of certain individuals. L. Y. Loring, "Report on Coyotero Apaches," unpublished manuscript.

Connor, Mrs. J. F., Englewood, New Jersey. Collection of Britton Davis's correspondence, including material from Thomas Cruse, George Morgan, George Converse, and others pertaining to period here included.

Huntington Library, San Marino, California. Papers of Walter S. Schuyler, including letters from Crook. A. H. Nickerson, "Major General George Crook and the Indians," unpublished manuscript.

Rutherford B. Hayes Memorial Library, Fremont, Ohio. Collection of hundreds of Crook documents, including *Annual Reports*, official correspondence, and other papers.

United States Government. National Archives and Records Service, Old Military Records Branch: *Apache Troubles*, 1879–83, Document File 4327-1881, Record Group 94; Adjutant General's Office, Letters Received, 1881–83; Department of Arizona, and District of New Mexico, Letters Sent, 1881–83; Letters Received, 1881–83; Military Division of the Pacific, Letters Sent, 1881–83; Letters Received, 1881–83; *Annual Report*, General of the Army, with subsidiary *Annual Reports* from pertinent subordinate commanders, 1881–83. Social and Economic Records Division (Department of Interior, Bureau of Indian Affairs), Letters Sent, Arizona Superintendency, 1875; Letters Received, Arizona, 1882. *House Report 1084*, 1914, "Indian War History of the Army During the Years 1865–1886, compiled from War Department Records"; *House Exec. Doc. I*, 49 Cong., 2 sess., serial 2460, "Papers Relating to the Foreign Relations of the United States (Mexico)," 570–691; *House Exec. Doc. I*, 50 Cong., 1 sess., serial 2532, "Papers Relating to

Foreign Relations," 692; *Senate Report 756,* 53 Cong., 3 sess., serial 3288; *Senate Exec. Doc. 88,* 51 Cong., 1 sess., "Letter from Secretary of War Transmitting Correspondence Regarding Apache Indians"; *Senate Exec. Doc. 117,* Parts I and II, 49 Cong., 2 sess.
United States Military Academy Library, West Point, New York. John G. Bourke Diary, 126 manuscript volumes.

GOVERNMENT PUBLICATIONS

American Decorations: A List of Awards of the Congressional Medal of Honor the Distinguished-Service Medal, Awarded under Authority of the Congress of the United States: 1862–1926. Washington, Government Printing Office, 1927.
Bourke, John G. "Medicine-Men of the Apache," Bureau of American Ethnology *Ninth Annual Report* (1892), 443–603.
Centennial of the United States Military Academy at West Point, New York, 1802–1902. 2 vols. Washington, Government Printing Office, 1904.
Chronological List of Actions, &c., with Indians, from January 1, 1866, to January, 1891. Washington, Adjutant General's Office, 1891.
Crook, George. *Resumé of Operations Against Apache Indians, 1882–1886.* Washington, Government Printing Office, 1887.
Heitman, Francis Bernard. *Historical Register and Dictionary of the United States Army, from its Organization, September 29, 1789, to March 2, 1903.* 2 vols. Washington, Government Printing Office, 1903.
Hodge, Frederick Webb. *Handbook of American Indians North of Mexico.* 2 vols. Washington, Government Printing Office, 1907.
Medal of Honor Recipients: 1863–1963, Prepared for the Sub-committee on Veterans' Affairs of the Committee on Labor and Public Welfare, United States Senate. Washington, Government Printing Office, 1964.
Mooney, James. *The Ghost-Dance Religion and the Sioux Outbreak*

181

of 1890, Bureau of American Ethnology *Fourteenth Annual Report* (1870). Reprint, Chicago, University of Chicago Press, 1965.

Record of Engagements with Hostile Indians Within the Military Division of the Missouri, from 1868 to 1882, Compiled from official records. Washington, Government Printing Office, 1882.

Royce, Charles C. "Indian Land Cessions in the United States," Bureau of American Ethnology *Eighteenth Annual Report* (1899), 521–964.

Swanton, John R. *The Indian Tribes of North America.* Bureau of American Ethnology *Bulletin 145.* Washington, 1953.

United States Statutes at Large. Vols. XXII, XXIII.

NEWSPAPERS

Florence–Tucson, Arizona, *Arizona Enterprise.*
Los Angeles, California, *Los Angeles Times.*
New York, New York, *New York Herald.*
New York, New York, *New-York Tribune.*
Prescott, Arizona, *Prescott Weekly Courier.*
Silver City, New Mexico, *Silver City Enterprise.*
Tombstone, Arizona, *Tombstone Epitaph.*
Tucson, Arizona, *Arizona Star.*

PRIMARY SOURCES

Betzinez, Jason. *I Fought with Geronimo.* Harrisburg, Pa., Stackpole Company, 1959.

Bourke, John G. *An Apache Campaign in the Sierra Madre.* New York, Charles Scribner's Sons, 1886. New Printing, 1953.

———. *On the Border With Crook.* New York, Charles Scribner's Sons, 1891.

Cook, James H. *Fifty Years on the Old Frontier.* New Haven, Yale University Press, 1923.

Crook, George. *General George Crook: His Autobiography.* Ed. by

Martin F. Schmitt. Norman, University of Oklahoma Press, 1946. New ed., 1960.

Cruse, Thomas. *Apache Days and After.* Caldwell, Idaho, Caxton Press, 1929.

Davis, Britton. *The Truth About Geronimo.* New Haven, Yale University Press, 1929.

Forsyth, George A. *Thrilling Days in Army Life.* New York, Harper & Brothers, 1900.

Horn, Tom. *Life of Tom Horn: A Vindication.* Denver, The Louthan Company, 1904. Privately printed.

Mazzanovich, Anton. *Trailing Geronimo.* 3d. ed. Hollywood, privately printed, 1931.

Rope, John, as told to Grenville Goodwin. "Experiences of an Indian Scout," *Arizona Historical Review,* Vol. VII, Nos. 1, 2 (January, April, 1936), 31–68; 31–73.

SECONDARY SOURCES

Bancroft, Hubert Howe. *History of Arizona and New Mexico.* San Francisco, The History Company, 1889.

———. *History of the North Mexican States and Texas.* 2 vols. San Francisco, The History Company, 1884, 1889.

Barnes, Will Croft. *Arizona Place Names.* Tucson, University of Arizona, 1935; 2d ed., rev. and enl., by Byrd H. Granger, University of Arizona Press, 1960.

Brandes, Ray. *Frontier Military Posts of Arizona.* Globe, Dale Stuart King, Publisher, 1960.

———ed. *Troopers West: Military & Indian Affairs on the American Frontier.* San Diego, Frontier Heritage Press, 1970.

Carter, W. H. *From Yorktown to Santiago with the Sixth Cavalry.* Baltimore, The Lord Baltimore Press, 1900.

———. *The Life of Lieutenant General Chaffee.* Chicago, University of Chicago Press, 1917.

Clum, Woodworth. *Apache Agent.* Boston, Houghton Mifflin and Company, 1936.

Cullum, George Washington. *Biographical Register of the Officers and Graduates of the U.S. Military Academy at West Point, N.Y.* 8 vols. Boston, Houghton Mifflin and Company, 1891–1910.

Diccionario Porrua: Historia, Biografia y Geografia de Mexico. 2d ed. Mexico City, Libreria Porrua, 1965.

Dictionary of American Biography. 22 vols. New York, Charles Scribner's Sons, 1958.

Dunn, J. P., Jr. *Massacres of the Mountains.* New York, Archer House, Inc., n.d.

Erwin, Allen A. *The Southwest of John Horton Slaughter: Cattleman, Sheriff.* Glendale, California, Arthur H. Clark Company, 1965.

Glass, Major E. L. N., comp. and ed. *The History of the Tenth Cavalry: 1866–1921.* Tucson, Acme Printing Company, 1921.

Hinton, Richard G. *The Handbook to Arizona.* San Francisco, Payot Upham & Company, 1878. Reprint. Tucson, Arizona Silhouettes, 1954.

History of Arizona Territory Showing Its Resources and Advantages; With Illustrations. No author cited. San Francisco, W. W. Elliott & Co., 1884. Reprint. Flagstaff, Northland Press, 1964.

King, James T. *War Eagle: A Life of General Eugene A. Carr.* Lincoln, University of Nebraska Press, 1963.

Leckie, William H. *The Buffalo Soldiers: A Narrative of the Negro Cavalry in the West.* Norman, University of Oklahoma Press, 1967.

Lockwood, Frank C. *The Apache Indians.* New York, The Macmillan Company, 1938.

———. *Arizona Characters.* Los Angeles, The Times-Mirror Press, 1928.

———. *More Arizona Characters.* Tucson, University of Arizona, 1943.

McClintock, James H. *Arizona: Prehistoric, Aboriginal, Pioneer, Modern.* 3 vols. Chicago, S. J. Clarke Publishing Company, 1916.

Marshall, James. *Santa Fe: The Railroad that Built an Empire.* New York, Random House, 1945.

Mullane, William H. *Indian Raids, as Reported in the Silver City Enterprise, Silver City, New Mexico: 1882–1886.* Silver City, The Enterprise, 1968.

————. *This is Silver City, New Mexico: 1882–1883–1884.* Silver City, The Enterprise, 1963.

National Cyclopedia of American Biography. 20 vols. New York, James T. White & Company, 1898–1926.

Ogle, Ralph Hedrick. *Federal Control of the Western Apaches: 1848–1886.* Albuquerque, University of New Mexico Press, 1940.

Opler, Morris Edward. *An Apache Life-Way: The Economic, Social, and Religious Institutions of the Chiricahua Indians.* New York, Cooper Square Publishers, Inc., 1965.

Pearce, T. M., ed., assisted by Ina Sizer Cassidy and Helen S. Pearce. *New Mexico Place Names: A Geographical Dictionary.* Albuquerque, University of New Mexico Press, 1965.

Rickey, Don, Jr. *Forty Miles a Day on Beans and Hay.* Norman, University of Oklahoma Press, 1963.

Roca, Paul M. *Paths of the Padres Through Sonora.* Tucson, Arizona Pioneers' Historical Society, 1967.

Thrapp, Dan L. *Al Sieber, Chief of Scouts.* Norman, University of Oklahoma Press, 1964.

————. *The Conquest of Apacheria.* Norman, University of Oklahoma Press, 1967.

Twitchell, Ralph Emerson. *The Leading Facts of New Mexican History.* 2 vols. Albuquerque, Horn & Wallace, Publishers, 1963.

Wallace, Ernest. *Ranald S. Mackenzie on the Texas Frontier.* Lubbock, Texas, West Texas Museum Association, 1964.

Wellman, Paul I. *The Indian Wars of the West.* New York, Doubleday and Company, 1947.

Wharfield, H. B. *Cooley: Army Scout, Arizona Pioneer, Wayside Host, Apache Friend.* El Cajon, California, privately printed, 1966.

Whitman, S. E. *The Troopers: An Informal History of the Plains Cavalry, 1865–1890.* New York, Hastings House Publishers, 1962.

Who Was Who. Chicago, The A. N. Marquis Company, 1943.

Willson, Roscoe. *Pioneer and Well Known Cattlemen of Arizona.* 2 vols. Phoenix, Valley National Bank, 1951, 1956.

Wilson, Neill C., and Frank J. Taylor, *Southern Pacific: The Roaring Story of a Fighting Railroad.* New York, McGraw-Hill Book Company, 1952.

ARTICLES AND ESSAYS

Barnes, Will Croft. "The Apaches' Last Stand in Arizona," *Arizona Historical Review,* Vol. III, No. 4 (January, 1931), 36–59.

Bourke, John G. "General Crook in the Indian Country," *Century,* Vol. XLI, No. 5 (March, 1891), 643–60.

Brinckerhoff, Sidney B. Book review, *The Journal of Arizona History,* Vol. IX, No. 1 (Spring, 1968), 48–52.

Clum, John P. "Apache Misrule," *New Mexico Historical Review,* Vol. V, Nos. 2, 3 (April, July, 1930).

———. "Geronimo," *New Mexico Historical Review,* Vol. III, Nos. 1, 2, 3 (January, April, July, 1928).

Farmer, Malcolm F. "New Mexico Camps, Posts, Stations and Forts," Santa Fe, compiled and mimeographed under direction of the Library, Museum of New Mexico, n.d.

Frank Leslie's Illustrated Newspaper, no author, June 2, 1883, "General Crook's Apache Campaign," 233.

Hanna, Robert. "With Crawford in Mexico," *Arizona Historical Review,* Vol. VI, No. 2 (April, 1935), 55–65.

Hodge, Frederick W. "In Memoriam: John Gregory Bourke," *Journal of American Folklore,* Vol. IX, No. 33 (April–June, 1896), 139–42.

Lyon, Juana Fraser. "An Apache Branch of Clan MacIntosh," *Clan Chattan,* Vol. IV, No. 2 (January, 1961), 15–18.

———. "Archie McIntosh, the Scottish Indian Scout," *Journal of Arizona History*, Vol. VII, No. 3 (Autumn, 1966), 103–22.

Middleton, Hattie (Mrs. G. M. Allison). Account of Indian Fight in Pleasant Valley (no title). *Frontier Times*, June, 1928, reprinted: *True West*, Vol. XI, No. 4 (March–April, 1964), 28, 48, 50.

Mulligan, R. A. "Apache Pass and Old Fort Bowie," *The Smoke Signal*, Tucson, Tucson Corral of the Westerners, No. 11 (Spring, 1965), 1–24.

Nalty, Bernard C., and Truman R. Strobridge, "Captain Emmet Crawford, Commander of Apache Scouts: 1882–1886," *Arizona and the West*, Vol. VI, No. 1 (Spring, 1964), 30–40.

Rush, Rita. " 'El Chivero'—Merejildo Grijalva," *Arizoniana*, Vol. I, No. 3 (Fall, 1960), 8–10.

Shipp, Lieutenant W. E. "Captain Crawford's Last Expedition," *Journal of the United States Cavalry Association*, Vol. XIX (October, 1905), 280ff.

Smith, Cornelius C. "The Fight at Cibicu," *Arizona Highways*, Vol. XXXII, No. 5 (May, 1956), 2–5.

Thrapp, Dan L. "Dan O'Leary, Arizona Scout," *Arizona and the West*, Vol. VII, No. 4 (Winter, 1965), 287–98.

Williamson, Dan R. "Al Sieber, Famous Scout of the Southwest," *Arizona Historical Review*, Vol. III, No. 4 (January, 1931), 60–76.

Woodward, Arthur. "Side Lights on Fifty Years of Apache Warfare 1836–1886," *Arizoniana*, Vol. II, No. 3 (Fall, 1961), 3–14.

INDEX

189

29–31; investigation of attack,
43–45
Fort Apache Reservation, Ariz.: 5, 9
& n., 43, 98
Fort Bayard, N.M.: 36
Fort Bowie, Ariz.: 33, 62, 72, 83, 84,
109, 110
Fort Cummings, N.M.: 8, 70
Fort Davis, Tex.: 61
Fort Grant, Ariz.: 4, 33, 41, 47, 53,
54–55, 56, 73
Fort Huachuca, Ariz.: 33, 62
Fort Lowell, Ariz.: 46
Fort McDowell, Ariz.: 33, 99, 103
Fort Stanton Reservation, N.M.:
9 & n.
Fort Thomas, Ariz.: 15, 28, 32, 43,
46–47, 53, 58, 72, 97, 109, 110, 119,
122
Fort Verde, Ariz.: 33, 34, 35, 99, 103
Fort Walla Walla, Wash.: 36
Fort Whipple, Ariz.: xv, 10, 15, 35,
125
Fort Wingate, N.M.: 33
Franco, Ygnacio: 93
Free, Mickey: 128, 140, 152; reports
Carr's command destroyed, 28; as
interpreter, 154; at Crook's con-
frontation, 156
Frelinghuysen, Frederick T.: 126
Fronteras, Sonora: xii
Fuero, Carlos: 60

Galeyville, Ariz.: 85, 87
Galicia, Jesús: 93
Gar (Apache): 43, 98
García, Lorenzo: ix, xiv, xvii, 116,
121, 160, 167, 169–70, 173; fight
with Loco, 91–93; Forsyth con-
frontation, 93–95; attacks Strong-
hold, 141–42
Garvey, Thomas: 60
Gatewood, Charles B.: 128, 140, 169
George (Apache): 45, 46, 48; his
band at Cibecue, 43; in Fort
Apache attack, 44; bolt of, 49ff.

Geronimo: xvi, 49, 50, 60, 77, 80, 92,
97, 113, 119, 140, 146, 154, 160, 163,
164, 165, 173, 178; as clairvoyant,
146–47; return of raiders, 154–56;
confronts whites, 159; plans treachery,
161–62; confers for last time, 168;
comes in, 176
Ghost dances: 11–12 & n.
Gidell (killed by Indians): 53
Gila River: 71, 75, 78, 80, 83, 113
Gleason (killed by Indians): 100
Globe, Ariz.: 33, 99, 100
Gordon, Charles G.: 30, 84
Grant, Ulysses S.: 37
Grierson, Benjamin Henry: 7
Grijalva, Merejildo: 41 ff., 41 n.,
121–22
Guadalupe, Sonora: xii
Guadalupe Canyon, Sonora: 73
Guadalupe Mountains, Sonora: 57
Guaymas, Sonora: xii, xiii, 111, 124
Guilfoyle, John F.: 8
Guzman Lake, Chihuahua: 60

Hackney, Aaron H.: 67
Hall, Charles S.: 73
Haskell, Harry L.: 35, 45, 46, 50, 77,
83–84
Hatch, Edward: 6–7, 12, 58, 68
Hentig, Edmund C.: 18, 23, 30; slain
at Cibecue, 24–25; body muti-
lated, 42
Hermosillo, Sonora: xii, 111
Heron, Major: 93
Hinkler, E.: 29
Hoag, Ezra: 46, 49, 50
Hopkins (packer): 135
Horn, Tom: 84–85, 85n., 128
Horseshoe Canyon, N.M.: xvii, 80,
81–82, 82–83n., 94; Loco engage-
ment, 81–83
Houdon, Louis: 100
Howard, Charles: 63–67, 74
Howard, Oliver Otis: 63, 113

Huachinera, Sonora: xvii, 135–36 & 135n., 138
Hurrle, Charles: 10–11 & n., 18, 97, 107; interprets at Cibecue, 20–22

Indian "ring": 113, 177

Janos, Chihuahua: xvi, 8, 68, 71, 93, 110, 136, 168, 169, 171
Jeffords, Thomas: 50–51, 71
Juh: vii, 12, 49, 62, 92, 97, 113, 140, 164; bolt of, 50–57; leadership of, 55 & n.; brings hostiles north, 74–75; takes Loco's people south, 76ff.; never surrenders, 163

Kah-thli (Apache): 121
Ka-ya-ten-nae (Apache): 91, 159–60, 162, 164, 176
Keogh, Pat: 84, 89
King, James S.: 34
Kingsbury, Henry P.: 34
Kirkwood, Samuel Jordan: 63

Las Vegas, N.M.: xii
Lincoln, Robert Todd: 101
Livingston, Edward D.: 25
Loco: vii, ix, xvii, 74, 96, 97, 154, 160; bolts, 76ff.; fight at Horseshoe Canyon, 81–83; Enmedio fight, 89–90; García fight, 91–95; losses, 94–95; surrenders to Crook, 162–63; returns with Crook, 164; Loco's people come in, 172–73
Lordsburg, N.M.: 7, 80, 94, 116
Loring, L. Y.: 4
Loud, John S.: xiii
Lugo, Serapio: 93

McComas, Charlie: 116
McComas, H. C.: 116
McCreery, George: 18
McDonald, David N.: 60; scout against Loco, 81
MacDonald, John F.: 20; shoots medicine man, is wounded, 25

McDowell, Irvin: 18, 22–23, 36, 38, 40, 41
MacGowan, Alexander B.: 31 & n., 97, 98
McIntosh, Archie: 51, 128, 140
Mackay, James O.: 128, 140
Mackenzie, Ranald S.: 36, 60, 61, 62, 68–70, 72, 74, 80–81, 95, 96, 126; ordered to Arizona, 36ff.; description of, 37–39; command in Juh outbreak, 51–58; methods, 105
McLellan, Curwen B.: 33, 56
McMillenville, Ariz.: 35, 100
Mangas (Apache): 176
Mangas Coloradas: 64
Map of Crook expedition: viiiff.; origin of, x–xii; drafting of, xiii
Martin, James P.: 172, 174
Meadows, John: 100
Mescalero Apaches: 62, 63
Mexican prisoners: 160
Mexico City: xii, 13, 113, 126
Middleton Ranch, Ariz.: 42–43
Miller, William: 26
Mills, Stephen C.: 84, 89
Moctezuma, Sonora: 137, 141
Mogollon Rim, Ariz.: 34, 100
Mohave Indians: 70
Monach, Frank: 135
Montoya, Ramon: 121–23
Moore, Lamar: ixff.
Morley, William Raymond: xii
Mosby (Apache): 43–44
Mose (Apache): 17, 22; defends medicine man, 19
Mount Graham: 54
Mule Pass, Ariz.: 57
Muntz, A. P.: xiv, xv
Murphy, Simon: xi

Nachez (Apache): 12, 49, 50, 62, 74, 91, 150, 159, 175
Nana (Apache): 7, 68; raid of, 8–9; reported at Cibecue, 39–40 & 40n.; meets Crook, 162; returns with Crook, 164

Na-ti-o-tish (Apache): 45, 75, 96;
at Cibecue and later, 42ff.; con-
tacted by Juh, 97–98; killed at Big
Dry Wash, 99–100
Navaho Indians: 11, 42, 64, 97
Navajo Bill (Apache): 159; spy
party to Mexico, 109–11
Ne-big-ja-gy (Apache): 42ff.
New York Herald: 137, 171–72
New-York Tribune: 170–71, 174–75
Nobles, Charles (Nat): 18, 32
Noch-ay-del-klinne (Apache): 3, 12,
17, 19, 42; life of, 3–4; dances,
10ff.; arrest ordered, 13ff.; Carr
confronts, 20ff.; killed, 25–27, 27n.
Nodeski (Apache): 119, 122; incor-
rigibility of, 119
Nogales, Ariz.: xii, 111
Norvell, John M.: 34
Notzin (Apache): 29

O'Leary, Dan: 34ff., 56
Opata Indians: 133
Opler, Morris E.: 147
Oputo, Sonora: 136
Overton, Gilbert E.: in Juh pursuit,
51–55
Owl: 137

Pack trains: 128; Crook's concern
for, 103–104
Pah-na-yo-tishn (Apache): *see*
Peaches
Palomas Lake, Chihuahua: 7, 68
Pangburn, S.D.: 97, 99
Payson, Ariz.: 34
Peaches (Apache): 118, 124; cap-
tured, 119; interviewed by Crook,
119–23; guides Crook, 128–39
Pedro (Apache): 28, 29, 43; band's
part in Cibecue affair, 41–42; in
attack on Fort Apache, 44–45
Peloncillo Mountains, N.M.: 87, 88,
173
Perry, David: 72, 73–74, 83, 84, 87,
99

Pinery Creek, Ariz.: 87
Pleasant Valley, Ariz.: 29, 34, 42–43
Prescott, Ariz.: 10
Price, William Redwood: 33ff., 53;
ordered to San Carlos, 35

Rada, Antonio: 93
Rafferty, William C.: 110, 175–76;
Loco pursuit and fight, 84–90
Raguero, Ramon: 125, 127, 167
Railroad Pass, Ariz.: 121
Randall, A. Frank: 137, 137–38n.,
139, 171
Reyes, Bernardo: 93, 111
Richmond, N.M.: *see* Virden
Río Grande: 8, 61
Robinson, Albert Alonzo: xiii
Romero, Matías: 112, 126
Roosevelt Dam, Ariz.: 54
Rope, John (Apache): xvi, 129,
134n., 170, 175; chronicles Sierra
Madre expedition, 129–39;
rancheria attack, 140–46; Apache
negotiations, 150–55; Crook's
meeting with chiefs, 155–58; re-
ports planned treachery, 160–62
Ross, Frank: 100

Sacramento Mountains, N.M.: 8
Safford, Ariz.: 122
Sagotal (Apache): 77
Salt River, Ariz.: 34
Samaniego (merchant): 134, 173
Samaniego, Bartolo: 53
Samaniego, Mariano: 125
San Bernardino, Ariz.: xii, 56, 57, 73,
131 & n., 173
San Bernardino River, Sonora: 132
San Carlos Reservation, Ariz.: 4, 5,
9n., 33, 34, 42ff., 50–51, 57, 61–62,
70, 72, 74, 75, 97ff., 109, 110, 112ff.,
118, 121ff., 150, 154, 160, 164–65;
Price takes over, 35; contacts with
hostiles, 63; Howard study of,
63–67; Loco's people bolt, 76ff.
San Carlos River, Ariz.: 46